T0331030

'This is an immensely accessible discussion of what it might be to be a team coach. Paul has drawn on a significant body of research and on his own extensive experience to guide the reader through a process of finding out for themselves what they want their practice to stand for. The contribution is significant in terms of helping the development of a rapidly expanding practice at the same time as drawing attention to the value of reflexivity in the practice of team coaching. The whole is presented in everyday language with practical, and highly relatable, examples.'

Dr Peter Jackson, *Director International Centre for Coaching & Mentoring Studies, Oxford Brookes Business School*

The Wise Team Coach

Based on three years of meta-research into team effectiveness and coaching, this book explores some of the most common contradictions and debates around the topic of team coaching and presents readers with a framework to enable them to explore this field for themselves, reflecting on their own experience and drawing their own conclusions.

Team coaching in organisations is still a relatively new discipline, with industry associations having only recently defined their first attempts to frame team coaching in the form of standard skills and competencies. As a new discipline we still see multiple perspectives on what team coaching is, and how it should best be practiced. The literature abounds with paradox and contradictions. Within this book Lawrence delves into these contradictions and debates, providing a framework to encourage readers to construct their own practice model.

Covering both theory and practical application, this will be a useful guide for both experienced team coaches and those entering the field.

Dr Paul Lawrence enjoyed a long corporate career, leading teams and businesses in the UK, Spain, Portugal, Australia, and Japan. Paul has been working as a coach and consultant since 2007, based in Sydney, Australia, and is a research associate at Oxford Brookes University in the UK.

The Wise Team Coach

Crafting a Personal Approach to Team Coaching

Dr Paul Lawrence

Routledge
Taylor & Francis Group

LONDON AND NEW YORK

Designed cover image: Getty Images

First published 2025
by Routledge
4 Park Square, Milton Park, Abingdon, Oxon, OX14 4RN

and by Routledge
605 Third Avenue, New York, NY 10158

Routledge is an imprint of the Taylor & Francis Group, an informa business

British Library Cataloguing-in-Publication Data
A catalogue record for this book is available from the British Library

Library of Congress Cataloging-in-Publication Data
Names: Lawrence, Paul, 1963–, author.
Title: The wise team coach : crafting a personal approach to team coaching /
Paul Lawrence.
Description: Abingdon, Oxon ; New York, NY : Routledge, 2025. |
Series: Coaching psychology | Includes bibliographical references and index.
Identifiers: LCCN 2024042122 (print) | LCCN 2024042123 (ebook) |
ISBN 9781032900841 (hardback) | ISBN 9781032900834 (paperback) |
ISBN 9781003546108 (ebook)
Subjects: LCSH: Employees–Coaching of. | Teams in the workplace–Management. |
Organizational behavior. | Executive coaching.
Classification: LCC HF5549.5.C53 L39 2025 (print) |
LCC HF5549.5.C53 (ebook) | DDC 658.3/124–dc23/eng/20250109
LC record available at https://lccn.loc.gov/2024042122
LC ebook record available at https://lccn.loc.gov/2024042123

ISBN: 978-1-032-90084-1 (hbk)
ISBN: 978-1-032-90083-4 (pbk)
ISBN: 978-1-003-54610-8 (ebk)

DOI: 10.4324/9781003546108

Typeset in Times New Roman
by Newgen Publishing UK

Dedication

To Suzi Skinner, my loving partner, who has played such a key role in helping me to keep this egg warm. To my four beautiful kidlets: Charlotte, Callum, Cameron, and Ashleigh, to Brent, Adi, Jesse, and Ruth. To my mum and dad and brother. And to my closest friends and relations.

Contents

Acknowledgements

I'd like to thank everyone who played a role of any kind in helping to bring this book to life. I've already thanked Suzi Skinner, my partner, for her ongoing efforts in helping me work through and express these ideas effectively and for encouraging me every step of the way.

I'd like to thank Padraig O'Sullivan for helping me to work through some of the early work, and together with Carole, inviting me to their house in Gerroa for some thinking and reflection around the time of COVID. And to Ingo Susing for trying to facilitate us.

I'd like to thank Babette Graham, Sarah Hood, Emma Hodgson, Jo Hood, and Ida Huang, for their help in working out how to translate these materials into practical tools for leaders at KPMG Australia, when we were all coaches there.

I'd like to thank Peter Jackson, Suva Chattopadhyay, and Suzi for reading the whole book while still in development, helping me review, polish, and refine.

I'd like to thank the following coaches who trusted this work sufficiently to enrol in the first Team Leader Accreditation Manual (TLIM) cohorts: Dave Tams, Stuart Jenner, Mark Rosenberg, Jo Hood, Adam Smith, Cat Dunne, Suva Chattopadhyay, Gina McCredie, Nick Wai, Samantha Lam, Charmaine O'Brien, Marsha Acker, Kari McLeod, Janet Horton, Lisa Geerlings, Shilpi Joshi, Michael Cullen, Kylie Holyland, Ajay Kelkar, Roger Bray, Eva Kovacs, Rachel Russell, Jo Hall, and of course Suzi and Pod.

I'd to thank the following coaches who shared the material for Chapter Six on Purpose: Sue Fontannaz, Sean O'Leary, Tara Nolan, Fran Cormack, Josie McClean, Errol Benvie, Carolyn Stevens, Jennifer Campion, Allen Moore, Robert Salt, Geoffrey Abbott, Roderick Cross, Sue McDonnell, Adam Smith, Renee Holder, Ian Sampson, Andy Homer, Gavin Dagley, Anne Bartlett, Jane Porter, Stuart Jenner, Mark Rosenberg, Andrew Venables, Sarah Stokes, Ken Whitters, Susan Kroening, Allard de Jong, Rosie Sweetman, Carol Fogarty, Claudia Filsinger, Dave Tams, Karen Tweedie, Emma Hodgson, Sarah Brammier, Suva Chattopadhyay, Chris Jackson, Mark Burrell, Tammy Turner, Kieran White, Sylvie Benjamin, Sallie Grey, Irial O'Farrell, Katharine McLennan, Edna McKelvey, Ingrid Studholme, Sebastian Fox, Jo Hood, Nick Wai, Chip McFarlane, Cat Dunne, and again Suzi and Pod.

I'd like to thank everyone who allowed me to share early versions of these ideas at conferences and webinars, including Peter Jackson and Tatiana Bachkirova at the International Centre for Coaching and Mentoring Studies at Oxford Brookes Business School; Raija Salomaa, Annina Hukari, Minna Heikkila, Terhi Skankiakos, and the folks at the University of Jyvaskyla; Joel Monk at Coaches Rising; Fiona Day and the British Psychological Society; Smaranda Dochia and the AC Global team; Pauline Triggiani and team at AC NSW; Heike Aiello at ICF Germany; TL Green and Katie Norton at ICF Metro DC; Kaj Hellbom and Elina Koponen at BCI; Georgina Woudstra and Allard de Jong at the Team Coaching Studio; and the Australian Psychological Society.

I'd like to thank Genevieve Vignes for setting me up with my first team coaching assignment, and every team brave enough to let me work with them since.

And everyone else with whom I've ever had a conversation about team coaching.

Introduction

This is a different kind of book about team coaching. In this book I'm not going to try and tell you how you should go about coaching teams. In this book I attempt to provide you with a rationale and framework for building your own approach to team coaching.

I've written the book for anyone interested in coaching teams, including professional team coaches and team leaders. In the book I present a simple framework and a range of ideas, some straightforward, others less so. If some of the ideas seem too complex given your current role, then move on. Pick what feels relevant but stay focussed on the task at hand – which is to build your own approach to team coaching. You don't have to be an uber-experienced professional team coach to benefit from constructing your own practice model.

I've been a professional coach now for about eighteen years and have coached teams for much of that time. I have rarely coached more than one team at once because I find the work very challenging. I dedicate a lot more energy to coaching a team than is reflected in my coaching hours. I am continually challenging myself as to what I did last time out and contemplating what I will do differently next time. I sometimes wake up in the middle of the night with a great new insight I must write down before I forget. Something that happened yesterday that I didn't pay sufficient attention to, or a great new idea as to what I will do tomorrow.

I still remember my first team coaching session. I had been talking to colleagues about wanting to give it a go, exchanging ideas as to what I might do. I think one of my colleagues assumed I had more experience than I did, and she put me forward to coach a newly formed project team in an adult educational establishment, somewhere in country New South Wales. I had no idea what I was doing. I walked into the room with an intention to help them form some goals and to let them get on with it while I observed their dynamics and prepared to help them reflect on how they might work together more effectively. The team wasn't happy. They had been volunteered for the project team without being asked and many of them didn't feel they had time to dedicate to whatever the project team had been formed to achieve. It wasn't at all clear to them what they were supposed to be working on because the executive leadership team had been vague. They didn't trust the executive leadership team, they didn't all trust each other, and they didn't trust me. When I sat

DOI: 10.4324/9781003546108-1

back to watch them at work, they stopped talking and turned round. They wanted to know what I was doing, what I was writing, and what value I thought I was bringing. They didn't want me sitting observing them – they wanted guidance, structure, and some clues as to how they go about tackling this unclear hazy task they had been set.

I just about got out alive. That's what it felt like.

I could have given it all up then, but it struck me how much I had to learn and how much I wanted to learn it, whatever 'it' was. The project team were a generous group of people and they let me keep working with them for another ten months. We built trust with each other, and we all learned how to contribute better to the team. In the meantime, I read everything I could find on team coaching, which at the time wasn't much, and spent a lot of time talking to those of my colleagues who also worked with the teams, seeking to learn from them.

A few years later, in 2016, I asked 36 team coaches what they did[1]. I recall feeling most reassured by the people who told me that team coaching doesn't get any easier.

> Participants said it's hard to manage team process without being good at managing self. Insecurity can show up in the way the coach operates, by becoming enmeshed in the system for example, or else seeking to push it away. Effective team coaches need to manage their egos and be open to learning. The coach may need to get used to years of never feeling completely confident and capable.

I'm still in that space, as are many other team coaches I talk to, and I think a part of me at least has come to like being in that space. Over the years I have attended training programs, kept on reading and attending learning events, and kept on doing the work. One of the things I've learned over that period is that there exist multiple schools of thought as to the best way to go about coaching a team, and very little evidence as to what does and doesn't work in practice[2,3,4]. Of those differences in perspective some are quite significant, for example, the extent to which a team coach should pay attention to team dynamics. Some team coaches see their role almost exclusively in terms of helping a team work out how to better work together. Others say we are wasting our time working on team dynamics – help the team align around purpose, goals, and roles, and the dynamics will look after themselves. I find myself being asked time and again (most often by fellow coaches, less so clients) what the difference is between team coaching, team facilitation, team building, consulting, etc., and reading different people's answers to these questions. Not all those answers are the same, not all of them make sense to me, and few of them seem to have consulted the facilitators, team builders, and consultants to see if they agree. Those differences have becoming increasingly *un*clear to me, as have the rationales as to why I need to be able to differentiate between these supposedly distinct activities.

The more I coach and the more I read, the less aligned I think we all are as to the nature of the work we do and how to go about it. There *do* exist coalitions of people, gathered around a particular framework or methodology, who seem quite definite, but these coalitions don't all agree with each other. And in the meantime, I keep on doing the work and having some wonderful and some discomfiting experiences.

Recently I decided to enact a major overhaul of my approach to team coaching. I searched the reference libraries for every article I could find on team effectiveness and every popular book on team coaching, identifying areas of alignment, discord, and enlightenment. In the end I concluded that there is no single definitive best approach to team coaching. But more and more books continue to be published on team coaching, many advocating a particular approach. And we have seen the coaching associations launch their first team coaching competency frameworks and accreditation programs based on those competencies. It seems like the less certain I become, the more certain other people become. I am not the only one. I talk to more and more team coaches in my supervision practice who come confused by the plethora of advice, rules, and standard proficiencies that now exist.

I conclude from all this that there is no definitive, evidence-based, person or model who can tell us how best to coach teams, but there are lots of people, and now institutions, who keep trying. I am not going to add to the mix with this book. The premise of this book is that we need to chart our own journey.

This is not to advocate for anecdote and fluff. On the contrary it is to advocate for spending time on exploring our own thoughts, philosophies, and preferred ways of working, so that we become more self-aware and effective practitioners. And it is to get into the habit of questioning that emerging model with reference to what we see and hear in the world at large. It is to probe and challenge everything we are told – to exercise our finally honed abilities to apply critical thinking and reflect on our and others' ways of working.

I called the book the 'wise' team coach to try and capture a sense of being able to take a broad perspective on the team coaching industry, and all the various people connected with the industry, to plug into the conversations taking place across this industry and watch how those conversations evolve into prevailing norms and generic standards. To be able to better understand ourselves, and how our own beliefs and experiences shape the role we play in those conversations. And to be choiceful and purposeful, confident and capable, in the way we go about our work. And to be respectful and curious in our interactions with others in the team coaching space, even those who hold quite different opinions to us.

How to read the book

In Chapter One I review attempts to define team coaching as a discrete practice with its own specific, standard, set of skills and competencies. How fit for purpose is this quest for something simple, generic, and easy to understand? I compare that quest with a philosophy that says we will never be able to reduce something as complex as team coaching down to a single set of skills or competencies. Instead, we might think in terms of 'practical judgment', an active process of learning based on purposeful reflection on experience.

In Chapter Two I consider a nice simple framework, the 3Ps, that can help us articulate the evolution of our practical judgment. The 3Ps stand for:

Philosophy   What ideas, theories, frameworks, personal values, and experiences shape our approach?

Purpose   Why do we do the work?

Practice   What do we actually do as a team coach? What would a fly-on-the-wall observe us doing?

The 3Ps encourage us to be thoughtful and questioning, to clarify and grow our own perspective on team coaching.

In Chapter Three I review some of the debates I came across in my journeys across the literature, podcasts, webinars, and events. I encourage you as you consider these debates to conduct your own research, formal or informal, to challenge what you hear, rather than take for granted what others may tell you is the right answer.

In Chapter Four I return to the world of team coaching competencies, definitive perspectives on what team coaching is and how it should be performed. What position do these competency frameworks take on the areas of debate framed in Chapter Three? I compare and contrast team coaching competency frameworks from three global coaching associations. What insights will that comparison generate for you in reviewing your relationship with team coaching?

By now I hope you are starting to think seriously about your 3Ps. In Chapter Five I share with you ten cool ideas I came across in my trawl of the team effectiveness literature. Some of these ideas may resonate for you and find a place in your team coaching **philosophy**. Even just a consideration of these ideas may encourage you to go and search for other ideas and theories to feed your thinking.

In Chapter Six I encourage you to explore your **purpose**. Why do you do this work? It isn't easy, so why do you do it? To help you I will l share the outcomes of an informal straw poll of 51 team coaches. Why do they do the work? How do their perspectives help you clarify your broad commitment to 'making a difference'?

In Chapter Seven I give you a practical example of how you might translate a philosophy into a **practice**.

By now I hope you will have a good idea as to what the 3Ps are and how they are helpful. In Chapter Eight I'll talk about supervision, one means by which to ensure you continue to grow and evolve as a team coach. Professional coaches will know what I mean by the phrase 'supervisor'. To me it doesn't mean someone watching over your shoulder telling you if you're doing it right or wrong. To me the coach supervisor is the person with whom you can reflect in continuing your ongoing journey toward excellence (however you choose to define excellence). If you are a team leader and you don't have access to professional supervision, then who else might you turn to as a thinking/doing partner in becoming a better team leader? And how might you best support those of your colleagues also striving to improve their capabilities in this area?

And then finally – some conclusions.

Enjoy the journey.

References

1. Lawrence, P. & Whyte, A. (2017). What do Experienced Team Coaches do? Current Practice in Australia and New Zealand. *International Journal of Evidence Based Coaching and Mentoring, 15(1)*, 94–113.
2. Peters, J. & Carr, J. (2019). What Does 'Good' Look Like? An Overview of the Research on the Effectiveness of Team Coaching. In: D. Clutterbuck, J. Gannon, S. Hayes, I. Iordanou, K. Lowe & D. Mackie (Eds.), *The Practitioner's Handbook of Team Coaching.* Routledge.
3. Hastings, R. & Pennington, W. (2019). Team Coaching: A Thematic Analysis of Methods Used by External Coaches in a Work Domain. *International Journal of Evidence Based Coaching and Mentoring, 17(2)*, 174–188.
4. Traylor, A.M., Stahr, E., & Salas, E. (2020). Team Coaching: Three Questions and a Look Ahead: A Systematic Literature Review. *International Coaching Psychology Review, 15(2)*, 54–68.

Chapter 1

Competencies and practical judgment

In this chapter I will share some perspectives on competencies and their role in assessing the ability of those who work with complexity. I will compare and contrast those perspectives with others who have written extensively on leadership and complexity, notably Ralph Stacey and his articulation of 'practical judgment'.

There are many vocations where it feels entirely appropriate to characterise the role in terms of skills and competencies. If I drive for a living, if I'm a builder, a dentist, a medic, or an accountant, then there are significant aspects of my role for which there are strict guidelines, things I need to be able to do and demonstrate to others that I can do. That is not to say that people in these professions may not occasionally come across situations which no one has come across before, but I imagine most of what these people do for a living demands easily defined skills, albeit skills that may be difficult to master. For each of these professions you must hold some form of licence and/or belong to an industry body that demands you prove your proficiency to practice.

No one has yet succeeded in persuading people that we need a mandatory global leadership association. Ralph Stacey would say that is a good thing. He points out that the way many of us think about leadership is very linear[1]. I might think, for example, that if I spend more time listening to your needs, then you will not want to leave my organisation and I have been a good leader. Recognising the limitations of that very linear way of thinking, I may recognise that whether you choose to stay in my organisation is subject to a range of factors, and I may need to do more than just listen to your needs. I may need to review your salary as well. The world is a bit more complicated. Though I have now recognised the situation is more complicated, I am still thinking of leadership in terms of levers and outcomes, the levers being the skills and competencies I need to demonstrate if I am to get good outcomes for my business.

Stacey then goes on to consider theories of complex adaptive systems. Through this lens no individual can reliably control the behaviour of another individual. The world is full of people, all interacting with each other all the time. What people think and do, emerges from a myriad of conversations taking place across an

DOI: 10.4324/9781003546108-2

extensive social network. So, I may spend more time listening to your needs and ask myself what sense you are making of those efforts?

- Do you perceive me to be genuinely interested? Or do you think I am trying to be a more skilful leader because I've been told to look interested?
- Does it matter to you whether I am interested in your needs? Perhaps you don't come to work to be understood, you just like to get on with the job. Or perhaps you have decided already that you don't think I am a very influential person within the organisation and my opinion doesn't matter very much.
- What other factors determine your interest in the company? Perhaps you have concerns about the way the company operates, its ethics and stance on sustainability issues. Perhaps you don't like the company's policy on working from home.

Whatever the case, I am not the only person who influences your views on all these things. You talk to colleagues, friends, and family. You may be a member of a social interest group or a political party. You read the news and magazines, listen to podcasts, and talk to your barista every morning when you stop to buy a coffee. We are all members of social networks, and we are all engaged in a constant series of conversations. Those conversations are ongoing and dynamic, as is the overall membership of the social network. And within that network people have power, different forms of power.

Many leaders recognise they have positional power, the authority to make certain decisions. They assume people look up to them and are bound to do as they are asked. But there are other forms of power too, for example, the extent to which I am well networked, both inside and outside the organisation. The extent to which people think I am a thought leader. The extent to which people just enjoy listening to me and are likely to agree with what I have to say. The extent to which I have access to certain resources, and so on. To influence anyone then, is complex. To attempt to influence a lot of people at once is even more complex. Having access to some generic skills and competencies may help me on occasion, it may be a useful place to start, but I won't get far with just my tool box of skills and competencies.

We can no more standardise situations than we can skills. For example, if I spend more time listening to your needs, exercising all my listening skills, and this matches your desire to be understood, then you may feel more engaged. But if you don't particularly want to be understood, if you prefer a more distant relationship where we just stick to the job at hand, me paying more attention to your needs may diminish your view of me as a leader.

What are we to do then if the challenges of our role are too complex to capture in a set of skills and competencies? Ralph Stacey writes about practical judgment[2]. Practical judgment is embedded in personal experience. It is a form of self-knowledge acquired through interaction with others. It cannot be taught as such, nor can it be reduced to a set of rules. Practical judgment is the experience-based ability to notice what's going on and to intuit what's most important about a situation. It is cultivated by doing the work and reflecting on that work with others. Competencies may be useful, but a rigid adherence to those rules blocks spontaneity and impedes the development of practical judgment. In other words, competencies may be useful *and* may get in the way of people becoming better leaders.

Nevertheless, many organisations place a lot of emphasis on skills. We have all seen generic leadership competency frameworks characterising the role of a leader in terms of a finite number of skills – usually something between six and eight. How are these frameworks useful? They won't help you become a great leader, but they may help you better navigate your organisation. They represent what someone in the organisation thinks leaders should be doing. That might be someone in HR, or it might be a leader or group of leaders. It's helpful to know what people in your organisation think leaders should be doing. Even more useful to explore where these frameworks came from. Who was engaged in putting them together? Who wasn't? What is it about these skills, at this moment in time, that led to their emergence? Probing as to where these skills came from may deliver some useful insights as to how your organisation works and how you might best navigate it. But don't assume everyone in the organisation thinks these are the right skills, and certainly don't assume that people in other organisations think the same way, despite how similar some leadership frameworks appear to be.

Don't assume everyone in your organisation thinks that the company competency frameworks are right. When I worked at BP, more than twenty years ago, we launched the first large-scale company-wide leadership program the company had ever designed. Before that, different divisions and geographies developed their own programs. As part of the exercise, we conducted large-scale surveys to determine how people around the organisation would decide whether our program was successful or not. We asked them what the critical attributes of a successful leader were, so we could track the evolution of those attributes over the course of the program. We analysed our data and found that our new version of these critical attributes bore no relation whatsoever to the company's existing leadership competency framework. That framework had been developed by HR in consultation with a few folks from senior leadership. It didn't reflect the views of the vast majority of employees.

And don't assume people across different organisations think the same way. Many of the people I have coached over the years have come to coaching because the behaviours that worked in their old company did not work in their new company. The ability to speak openly and clearly, for example, was valued in my old company, but isn't working in my new company – people think I'm aggressive and rude.

But many organisations persevere with this focus on competencies and skills. That may be helpful or not, depending on how they are positioned, but if they're being positioned as a complete depiction of what successful leaders do, then this is a gross simplification. The problem is that we do like to make things simple, without always acknowledging the risks of over-simplification.

Coaching

Unlike leadership, the coaching industry *has* determined standard competencies for all coaches to adhere to, though we have several to choose from because there is more than one coaching industry body. There are three big global industry associations. Coaching is different to the aforementioned vocations, in that coaches are not legally obliged to belong to any of these associations if they don't want to, though some associations encourage purchasers of coaching services to insist upon coaches being accredited.

Why the desire to have competencies for coaching and team coaching? Lucy Widdowson and colleagues suggest it is because standard competencies help organisations to assess coaches, provide a common framework for educating coaches, and provide a consistent basis for coach accreditation, something they say that purchasers of coaching services require[3]. But Tatiana Bachkirova and Carmelina Lawton Smith highlight various problems with trying to characterise good coaching solely in terms of competencies[4], some of which are included in articulating the following four issues:

1. The competency issue

I've talked already about skills and competencies in the context of leadership. The same applies to coaching. Just as Stacey suggested that a rigid adherence to skills frameworks can get in the way of the leader development, so Bachkirova and Lawton Smith argue that an over reliance on coaching competency frameworks *"oversimplifies coaching practice and expertise and stultifies more creative solutions"*. Standard competencies may i) miss important aspects of practice, ii) divert attention from other actions that may lead to similar or better outcomes, iii) misrepresent what experienced coaches do, iv) limit inquisitiveness and exploration, v) divert attention from critical thinking, and vi) direct coaches toward historically successful behaviours, now outdated.

Other authors have described how *little* guidance competency frameworks often provide. For example, what do the following coaching competencies look like in practice? At best, they seem open to interpretation:

- Is sensitive to clients' identity, environment, experiences, values, and beliefs.
- Uses awareness of self and one's intuition to benefit clients.
- Is comfortable in a space of not knowing.

Ralph Stacey talked about practical judgment. Qing Wang and colleagues talk about an effective coach having a different way of being[5]. David Drake compares novice coaches (learning the rules) to intermediates (breaking the rules) to masters (changing the rules) and to artisans (transcending the rules)[6]. Suzi Skinner and I explored what it means to be wise[7]. All these different perspectives suggest that the effective practitioner does more than adhere to a set of rules, which means they cannot be assessed solely in terms of standard generic competencies.

Standard competencies present a misleading picture to the potential purchaser of coaching services. They imply that everyone who coaches agrees with the list and coaches the same way. That just isn't true. I know lots of MCC accredited coaches, and many of them tell me they had to adapt their coaching style to become accredited. How they coached in the assessment is not how they coach in the real world. So having standard competencies doesn't ensure consistent behaviours. Coaches are all different and will always work differently. Adrian Myers and Tatiana Bachkirova asked experienced coaches to witness other coaches in action[8]. Coaches-in-action and clients were mostly happy with the coaching sessions, but observers were more critical. Observers appeared to be assessing the sessions through their own personal perspective as to what constitutes good coaching and were making untested assumptions as to the impact of the behaviours that they didn't like.

If there are multitude of coaches out there, coaching differently, and most seem to be doing so successfully, why do we continue to try, or pretend to try, to define some overarching 'gold standard' to which we are all bound to aspire?

2.   The multiple levels issue

When you go to your local surgery you may be interested in talking to a doctor with a particular speciality, but you don't tend to ask for an associate doctor, a practitioner doctor, or a master doctor. We assume that all qualified doctors know what they are doing. Yet in the coaching world we have defined different levels of 'expertise', often with reference to these somewhat dubious competencies. In the leadership world, I suggested that competency frameworks may be a useful reference point for new leaders seeking to understand what others believe to be the basics of their craft. But in the coaching world, by talking about different levels of competence, we imply that we don't need to look beyond skills and competency to define whatever we mean by 'mastery'. There exists no evidence whatsoever to suggest that 'master coaches' are better at coaching than novice coaches[9]. Studies exploring mastery all highlight the complexity of mastery, and none try to articulate that mastery solely in terms of skills and competencies. It is hard then not to be somewhat sceptical in wondering if these gradated schemas are not at least in part a consequence of the incremental revenues they generate for accrediting bodies, and the resistance of coaches who have gone to the considerable time and expense of attaining those accreditations, to having that status removed. And I say that as someone who is supposedly a 'master' coach and accredited 'master' team coach.

3.   The education issue

In professions such as medicine and law, for example, prospective practitioners must gain a qualification from a university. The people who deliver these programs are independent scholars, and programs are subject to independent state regulation and extensive peer review. Once students have completed their formal qualification, then they are obliged to start practising under supervision. Once they have qualified, then they are free to practice and there are no further levels of practice defined solely in terms of assessed competencies.

In the coaching world it is the coaching associations who decide whether a particular training program is appropriate, and in most cases the organisations delivering that training must pay the coaching association to have their programs accredited. These programs often focus more on skills and competencies, and less on theories and underlying assumptions, and only a tiny proportion of programs are offered by universities. There is no overarching body independent of the various industry associations questioning the quality of this training.

Training bodies are usually required to base their training on the industry association's competencies, but these competencies are not based on a strong evidence base. I recently participated in a workshop held as part of a wider process whereby one of the coaching associations reviewed their competencies. The association invited experienced coaches to come and share their perspectives as to what works and what doesn't work. A new set of coaching competencies was then agreed, based on the outcome of all the workshops. This consensus view constitutes evidence of a sort, but it isn't strong evidence. There exists little incontrovertible evidence for the impact of a particular skill or behaviour on coachee outcomes. Placing too much reliance on what coaches think works is problematic because there is evidence to suggest that coaches and coachees often have quite a different experience of the same coaching session, and a different perspective as to what it was the coach did that was most impactful. Coaching competencies, therefore, are largely grounded in the unsubstantiated opinions of coaches who have been around a long time, some of whom will have quite traditional perspectives on their work. A set of stories and myths that the resulting competency frameworks serve only to reinforce. That is not to discard those perspectives, only to realise their limitations.

4.   The philosophical issue

Building on the education issue, a skills and competency approach doesn't oblige the coach to think very hard about what they are doing and why. So long as the coach can put a series of defined skills and competencies into practice, then they don't need to apply any thought to any of the theories and philosophies underpinning these skills. This supposes that the 'unthinking coach' is as likely to succeed as a coach as the 'thinking coach'. Coaches are not asked to have any understanding of human psychology. Nor do they need to have any particular perspective on systems thinking and theories of change. They don't need to think about the models and frameworks they are presented with, nor challenge them. Returning to Ralph Stacey for a moment, Stacey didn't have a lot to say specifically about coaching, but he did say in one paper that one of the most important roles of a coach is to "explore how coach and client are thinking together about how they are *thinking*"[10]. A sole focus on skills and competencies leaves all the thinking to those who build the competencies.

I'd like to make three more points before moving on to the next chapter.

First, I'm not suggesting that coaching competencies are 'bad'. Many of the behaviours we see listed in coaching competencies are the kinds of behaviours we would expect coaches to be able to engage in, if called upon. Coaching competencies may be a useful way of welcoming novice coaches into the broader coaching community, helping them to understand what kinds of behaviours may be required of them. At the same time, we must recognise the limitations of standardised skills and competencies and encourage people to further explore their craft with energy, criticality, and a discerning mind. We must share perspectives on the importance of reflective practice (including coaching supervision). We must encourage people to see these lists of skills and competencies for what they really are (and really are not). And over time, we need to somehow manage our collective enthusiasm for defining different levels of excellence in terms that seem to serve little useful function.

The second point to make is that not all coaching accreditation bodies are the same. The big three all have coaching competencies and advocate for different levels of competence, but they place different levels of emphasis on the importance of those skills and competencies vs the value of practical judgment. We will see that more clearly in Chapter Four.

Third, not all coaches are members of coaching organisations nor learned how to be a coach at an industry training school. If you are one of those coaches, then this chapter may feel less relevant to you. You studied coaching and team coaching at a university perhaps, where the limitations of a competency-based approach were evident and there was an emphasis on critical thinking. You may already think in terms of 'practical judgment' or an alternative construct. If that's you, and you're not all that interested in what the coaching associations are up to, then I hope you will still find the rest of this book helpful in helping you further refine who you are as a team coach.

So then, what are we to do if we cannot rely solely on skills and competencies to define good practice? How do we operationalise 'practical judgment'? In Chapter Two I will talk about the 3Ps.

References

1. Stacey, R. (2012). *Tools and Techniques of Leadership and Management. Meeting the Challenge of Complexity.* Routledge.
2. Stacey, R. (2012). *Tools and Techniques of Leadership and Management. Meeting the Challenge of Complexity.* Routledge.
3. Widdowson, L., Rochester, L., Barbour, P., & Hullinger, A.M. (2020). Bridging the Team Coaching Competency Gap: A Review of the Literature. *International Journal of Evidence Based Coaching and Mentoring, 18(2),* 35–50.

4. Bachkirova, T. & Lawton Smith, C. (2015). From Competencies to Capabilities in the Assessment and Accreditation of Coaches. *International Journal of Evidence Based Coaching and Mentoring, 13(2)*, 123–140.
5. Wang, Q. (2013). Structure and Characteristics of Effective Coaching Practice. *The Coaching Psychologist, 9(1)*, 7–17.
6. Drake, D. (2011). What do Coaches Need to Know? Using the Mastery Window to Assess and Develop Expertise. *Coaching: An International Journal of Theory, Research and Practice, 4(2)*, 138–155.
7. Lawrence, P. & Skinner, S. (2023). *The Wise Leader. A Practical Guide for Thinking Differently About Leadership.* Routledge.
8. Myers, A. & Bachkirova, T. (2020). The Rashomon Effect in the Perception of Coaching Sessions and What This Means for the Evaluation of the Quality of Coaching Sessions. *Coaching: An International Journal of Theory, Research and Practice, 13(1)*, 92–105.
9. Bachkirova, T. & Lawton Smith, C. (2015). From Competencies to Capabilities in the Assessment and Accreditation of Coaches. *International Journal of Evidence Based Coaching and Mentoring, 13(2)*, 123–140.
10. Stacey, R.D. (2012). Comment on Debate Article: Coaching Psychology Coming of Age: The Challenges We Face in the Messy World of Complexity. *International Coaching Psychology Review, 7(1)*, 91–95.

Chapter 2

The 3Ps

If team coaching is too complex to rely solely upon generic skills and competencies, then what are we to do? In this chapter I outline a simple framework for defining your own approach to team coaching – the 3Ps.

The 3P framework was first articulated by David Lane in 2006 in talking broadly about supervision[1], before later being adapted to coaching supervision specifically, and coaching, by Tatiana Bachkirova, Peter Jackson, and colleagues[2,3,4]. You can use the framework to clarify your approach to pretty much anything. I have used it to help leaders clarify their approach to leadership. I have often wondered if I might have been a better dad had I used it earlier in life to clarify my approach to parenting.

The 3Ps stands for philosophy, purpose, and practice. Though we talk about philosophy, articulating your 3Ps doesn't need to be an intellectual exercise. I use it with new coaches, new leaders, new leader-coaches – it can be used by anyone. The degree to which it becomes theoretical depends on the extent to which your practice is informed by theory.

Philosophy

Don't be put off by the word 'philosophy'. I imagine we might be using a different word if we could find a word with similar meaning that also began with the letter P. Perspective perhaps? The big question here is: through what lens do you look at the world?[5] Your perspective/philosophy is informed, whether you realise it or not, by all your experiences as a human being, your personal values, and everything you have ever heard, read, or seen, about team coaching. Ask yourself:

- What experiences have been most pivotal in you becoming the team coach you are today?
- Which of your values show up in the way you operate?
- What theories and frameworks most inform your practice?

DOI: 10.4324/9781003546108-3

Experiences

I recall my very first team coaching session, approaching the session with nothing but curiosity, an open mind, and some trepidation. It was a brand-new team, and I discovered very quickly that the team wanted me to provide them with some kind of structure in order to feel safe. I struggled to give them what they wanted. Ever since I have paid special attention to what a team needs in order to feel safe.

I recall another early assignment which felt like it never got going. My initial contact was with the HR Director, and I found it hard to get into the CEO's diary to establish his commitment to the cause. The process eventually fizzled out without us ever gaining real clarity as to what everyone was trying to achieve, especially the CEO. Ever since I have placed a strong emphasis on contracting.

I recall another experience working with a team on building trust. The team absolutely engaged with a particular exercise in getting to know each other. I flexed the session objectives to make sure they had the time they needed because they wanted to spend more time talking to each other. Ever since I have been careful to re-contract with the team whenever it feels appropriate, and to pay special attention to the need for people to connect.

Values

What is really important to you? What behaviours in others trigger you and make you angry? If you have a strong value around people being heard and understood, then this may show up in the amount of time you spend working on relationships, and paying attention to anyone in the team whose voice isn't being heard. If you have a strong value around achievement, then you may spend more time helping the team to clarify its objectives, making sure those objectives are measurable, and encouraging people to hold each other to account. If you have a strong value around creativity, then you may pay most attention to the extent the team is successful in surfacing new ideas and approaches.

Theories and frameworks

I know a lot of coaches who were inspired by Patrick Lencioni's 'Five Dysfunctions of a Team'[6]. I know a lot of coaches whose work leans heavily upon other books or courses they attended. I know team coaches who started working with teams in a clinical environment, whose approaches are much informed by the theories they were taught there. Whose theories and ideas do you think have most influenced your practice?

To work through these questions requires a degree of self-awareness. When I ask coaches which theories and frameworks most inform their practice, the answer is often "*I'm eclectic. I know lots of theories and they all have an impact.*" You may well be eclectic, but are you aware which of the many theories, models and frameworks you have been exposed to are most integrated into the way you think about team coaching? Some years ago, I interviewed 36 team coaches, curious to discover what they all did[7]. Between them they referred to more than a hundred theoretical models and frameworks, including psychodynamic theories, adult development theories, systems theories, appreciative enquiry, structural dynamics, humanist psychology, Gestalt, etc. The question though is which of these ideas most resonate with you? And how do they influence your work? And do you understand why these theories have touched you most? This understanding will enable you to better define the work you do, further explore the work you do, and notice more clearly what other theoretical perspectives you might usefully further explore and integrate.

Purpose

Coaching teams isn't easy work. So why do you do it? In Chapter Six we'll see how more than 51 coaches answered that question recently in preparation for writing this book. This is about what you are trying to achieve as a team coach. What gives you most satisfaction in the work that you do?

Many people first answer this question by answering "*I do it to make a difference.*" OK, but what sort of difference? And why spend so much time helping to make a difference through working with teams? There are lots of other ways you could be seeking to make a difference in the world. Some people say simply that the purpose of their work is to help teams work together more effectively. In service of what? In service of personal wellbeing, team performance, or a general desire for harmony in the world?

The nature of our purpose has a fundamental impact on the work that we do. If my purpose is to enhance wellbeing, by helping people understand how to build a collaborative, nurturing work environment, then you will see me behaving differently to the team coach whose purpose is to help teams achieve more (regardless of levels of wellbeing). And both coaches may act differently to the team coach whose purpose is to help organisations become more effective by helping teams relate better with each other.

Practice

Finally, what do you *do*? If someone were to shadow you for a couple of months, what would they observe you doing:

- On first being asked if you'd be prepared to coach a team?
- In taking the initial brief?
- In seeking to understand the needs of different stakeholders?
- In preparing to meet members of the team for the first time?
- In session with a team?
- In responding should a team apparently disengage with you, or with each other?

Etc.

As we will see in Chapter Three, some aspects of practice are quite contentious. For example, do you work solely with the team or are you happy to work with individuals on the team at the same time? When, if at all, would you insist on bringing a co-coach into the room? When, if at all, would you consent to being a co-coach?

Integration

Once you've come up with a first draft of your 3Ps, ask yourself two questions:

1. How well does my model hang together?
2. To what extent is my focus balanced?

If we focus on each of the 3Ps as if they were quite different areas of enquiry, then we may miss unresolved discrepancies. If, for example, I say that I put great emphasis on contracting, based on my previous experiences as a team coach and the emphasis placed on contracting by my favourite writer on team coaching, but in describing my practice I have little to say about contracting, then what does that imply? Or I've focussed on my values around respect and people being heard, but in practice I talk only about the need to get aligned around purpose and objectives? Again, what does that imply?

And it may be helpful to look at how well our focus is balanced. If I've written just a paragraph on philosophy, and five pages on practice, recreating all my favourite methodologies and techniques, then what does that say about those methodologies and techniques? To what extent is my work thoughtful and considered, versus applying someone else's model without having considered the extent to which these processes are based on solid theoretical and ethical foundations?

Where to start?

David Lane's model started with Purpose, implying perhaps that one's philosophy is subservient to what you are trying to achieve. Tatiana Bachkirova and Peter Jackson start with Philosophy on the basis that my Philosophy ought to define my purpose. They also say it doesn't really matter. If we are curious and committed to learn, then our 3Ps will constantly evolve and change. The process will be iterative and ongoing. I may listen to a podcast one day and come across a brand-new idea whose philosophy I immediately embrace. Or I may one day realise that my purpose in doing the work has shifted, without me being aware. Or I may observe another team coach in action and see them practice a technique I want to use too. So, I suggest you start where you want to start, that you keep thinking about your 3Ps as part of your ongoing reflective practice, and that you keep an eye on the extent to which the whole is coherent (Figure 2.1).

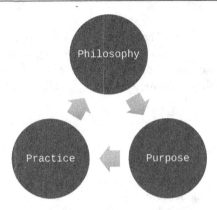

Figure 2.1 The 3Ps

All that said, in my experience some people struggle with articulating purpose, and sometimes skip that part of the model together. They suggest that their clients are most interested in what they do, and sometimes whose models they draw upon, but are rarely interested in understanding their purpose. But to be more aware of our purpose is to be more connected to our motivation for doing the work. It enables us to be more focussed and engaged. If you are struggling with the purpose question, then perhaps take the advice of Tatiana Bachkirova and Peter Jackson and start with philosophy. As we will see in Chapter Six, philosophy and purpose are inextricably intertwined.

The 4th P

The 3Ps framework is a reflective device to help you become clearer as to who you are as a team coach, and who you want to be. The difference between the two constitutes your ongoing action **plan** – the 4th P. A considered reflection of your 3Ps ought to lead you quite naturally to your 4th P. No matter how experienced or inexperienced you are, some of the following questions may be useful:

- Which of the models and frameworks you like do you want to explore further?
- What new models and theories do you want to explore?
- What will you read? What podcasts will you listen to? What training/events will you attend?
- Is there a value in further exploring how your values and experiences appear to be informing your practice?
- Based on your last couple of assignments, what do those experiences tell you about why you do the work?
- When you feel you've been successful, what was it that you did that made it successful?

- What experiments will you try in working differently?
- When will you make the time to reflect on these questions?
- Who will you reflect with?

A commitment to critical analysis, rigour, and being evidence-based

I once interviewed for an academic role working in a coaching school that was part of a bigger academic department. Most of the people interviewing me knew nothing about coaching, and as part of the process I was asked to present to a group of academics including professors, tutors, and research students. In that presentation I was asked to explain my approach to teaching, and so I shared the 3Ps. I hadn't got far before I was interrupted by an irate research student, whose objections were apparently shared by several of the folks sitting nearby judging by the nodding heads. They objected on the basis that scientists should be teaching material based only on hard-edged evidence. For them the role of the academic researcher/teacher was to establish the evidence for approaches and then teach those evidence-based approaches to students. To present the 3Ps and allow people to make their own minds up was to elude responsibility. People could make up any old rubbish and claim their views were valid.

The person who spoke with most passion was a pharmacist. He worked on developing new drugs, and a key part of his role was to prove that those drugs were safe to be used. I can see why he was aghast. To him I must have presented as a quack medic, someone like William J.A. Bailey, lauding the therapeutic benefits of Radithor in curing impotence and mental health disorders in the 1930s. Radithor was actually radium-226 and radium-228 dissolved in water and was radioactive. This student was committed to proving cause and effect and expected the same of anyone else working in his department. The problem, as I have pointed out already, is that the focus of coaching (and leadership) is on human relationship, and the way that we all think and behave is cultivated by a multitude of factors that are forever shifting and changing. The role of the academic in teaching coaching or leadership, I would argue, is to cultivate critical thinking, not to present solutions. The relevance and value of our 3Ps is linked to the quality of our reflection, which in turn is linked to our capacity to engage in critical thinking. Coaching a team is not like testing a new drug in a highly controlled, sterile environment. The environment is not sterile. There are numerous factors at play, many of them invisible. Nor can it be controlled, not if you view the world through a complex systemic lens. There is no set of rules we can rely on to do a great job. Instead, we must engage in a continuous process of experimentation and reflection.

The wise coach

I love to spend time with coaches. Coaches are, on the whole, lovely people, very empathetic and supportive. The flip-side of that is that some of us (certainly not *all* of us) are reluctant to challenge or to contradict. Yet if we see the world of team coaching for what it is, we see commonality, but we also see debate and discord. We can adopt a position, based on our own beliefs and experiences, indeed we probably will, but we can also seek to understand the sense that others are making. To be wise is to notice our own deeply held beliefs and to own where they come from. This requires us to ask questions, to challenge, and to share with others how we see the world. This desire to learn requires us to challenge what doesn't immediately make sense. Not because we want to embarrass someone or prove ourselves to be the smartest person in the room, but because we want to know. The committed learner doesn't take what they are told as gospel. He or she digs deep, probes, and seeks to understand.

- Where did you come up with that list of team coaching competencies? Tell me, please, in detail.
- What do you mean when you say your model is research-based?
- What do you mean when you say your approach is based on neuroscience? What neuroscience? Whose works? What papers?
- What do you mean when you say, "*most people agree that ...*". Which people? Which people *disagree*, and why?
- You say you are a systemic coach? What does that *mean*?

The last question is one I found myself asking a few years ago. I kept bumping into coaches telling me they were systemic. So, I asked them what they meant. Some people said it meant taking a balcony view. I wondered what that had to do with systems? Others said that they compared the work environment to the functioning of the human body. Others talked about the functioning of complex adaptive systems and weather systems. It was all very confusing and not very satisfying. I then possibly went a bit overboard in trying to pin down what it meant to be 'systemic'. I read a whole lot of work on systems theories and then published the findings[8], findings I will elaborate in the next chapter.

The point I want to leave you with here is that the 3Ps is not intended to be a simple, tick-box exercise. It is intended to be a difficult exercise, demanding that you get curious about yourself, your values and experiences, and your underlying purpose in life. It demands you to be curious, rigorous, and sceptical about all you are told about team coaching. Don't take what others say at face value. Probe, challenge, ask questions, and share perspectives.

Putting the time and effort into formulating your 3Ps and continuing to revisit your 3Ps on a regular and ongoing basis as part of your commitment to learning, this is the alternative to abiding to a set of competencies. The team coaching competencies presented to you by the various industry associations, authors, and training organisations may well have merit, but it's hard to say without exploring where they came from and how they were built. Be the wise coach, curious as to how these various frameworks evolved and determined to probe and understand

and learn, and ultimately decide for yourself how strong is the evidence underpinning these constructions? And while you engage in this ongoing process of learning and challenge, hold close the team coach you think you want to be, now, and in the future. The more work you put into the process, the more confident and capable you will be in your work.

References

1. Lane, D. (2006). *The Emergence of Supervision Models*. Presentation at the Annual Conference of the Special Group in Coaching Psychology of the BPS (unpublished).
2. Bachkirova, T. & Lawton Smith, C. (2015). From Competencies to Capabilities in the Assessment and Accreditation of Coaches. *International Journal of Evidence Based Coaching and Mentoring, 13(2)*, 123–140.
3. Bachkirova, T. (2016). The Self of the Coach: Conceptualization, Issues, and Opportunities for Practitioner Development. *Consulting Psychology Journal: Practice and Research, 68(2)*, 143–156.
4. Jackson, P. & Bachkirova, T. (2019). The 3Ps of Supervision and Coaching: Philosophy, Purpose and Process. In: E. Turner & S. Palmer. *The Heart of Coaching Supervision. Working with Reflection and Self-Care.* Routledge.
5. Jackson, P. & Bachkirova, T. (2019). The 3Ps of Supervision and Coaching: Philosophy, Purpose and Process. In: E. Turner & S. Palmer. *The Heart of Coaching Supervision. Working with Reflection and Self-Care.* Routledge.
6. Lencioni, P.M. (2002). *The Five Dysfunctions of a Team*. Jossey-Bass.
7. Lawrence, P. & Whyte, A. (2017). What do Experienced Team Coaches do? Current Practice in Australia and New Zealand. *International Journal of Evidence Based Coaching and Mentoring, 15(1)*, 94–113.
8. Lawrence, P. (2021). Team Coaching: Systemic Perspectives and their Limitations. *Philosophy of Coaching: An International Journal, 6(1)*, 52–82.

Chapter 3

Ten debates

In Chapter One I questioned the extent to which we can define team coaching solely in terms of skills and competencies. Attempting to define team coaching in such terms inevitably leads to us over-simplifying what is required to be an effective team coach. In Chapter Two I considered a nice simple framework that can help us to define our own personal approach to team coaching, an approach that resonates with our experiences and values.

As I said in the Introduction, I recently overhauled my approach to team coaching, reading more than 500 academic articles, various books and book chapters. In conducting that research, it became apparent to me how unaligned the team coaching community is in describing what we do and how we go about our work. I won't say misaligned, because that implies that it would be a good thing if we all agreed with each other. Right now, I'm not sure why we would all *want* to be aligned. Diversity of approach means diversity of thought and practice, challenge and innovation. So, let's embrace our diversity, whilst at the same time being wise, respectfully challenging ourselves and others.

In this chapter I share with you ten debates, ten areas where different people hold quite different views on team coaching. I don't ask you to immediately decide where you stand on each of the debates, though I do invite you to ultimately form a view. To arrive at that view may require you to talk to some people and do some of your own digging and probing. I apologise in advance if my own 3Ps reveal themselves in outlining these ten debates. If it feels like I'm being definitive, then of course challenge my thinking as much as you would anyone else's.

I start with some quite philosophical debates then segue into more tactical areas, areas of practice. The ten debates cover all aspects of our 3Ps, but the first six debates are perhaps primarily philosophical:

1. What is a team?
2. What does a team coach do – broad scope?
3. What does a team coach do – specific role?
4. How directive can a team coach be?
5. What about team dynamics?
6. What does it mean to be a systemic team coach?

DOI: 10.4324/9781003546108-4

What we think about the next four debates will depend on our philosophy *and* are fundamental from a practice perspective:

7. How big should a team be?
8. When is the right time to coach a team?
9. Is it OK to coach teams with part-time members?
10. Can I coach the team and individuals on the whole team at the same time?

Once I've outlined each of the debates, I'll return to the subject of wisdom, and provide an example of interrogating what we are told in service of deepening our understanding of an area. The example I've chosen is the sixth debate – what it means to be a systemic team coach.

1. What is a team?
This might seem like a strange one. A team is simply a group of people all brought together to achieve a long-term task – right? That is certainly the prevailing view, but there are some problems with this perspective, as we shall see.

Ruth Wageman and colleagues are notable proponents of the traditional view. They have, over the years, defined six conditions of team effectiveness[1], the first of which is that the team is a 'real' team, which means that:

*   The team has clear boundaries. Everyone knows who is a member and who is not.
*   Team members are interdependent for some common purpose, obliged to leverage each other's skills and experience to achieve that common purpose.
*   The team has some stability of membership. People have time to work out how best to work with each other.

Accordingly, Richard Hackman and Nancy Katz[2] wrote:

> Conventional wisdom about group stability is pessimistic about the viability and performance of groups whose members stay together for a long time. Conventional wisdom is wrong.
>
> Hackman and Katz (2010)

In other words, teams should not only be real, but the more stable the team, the more successful it is likely to be. Through this lens, to create a real team takes careful thought and planning. The most powerful interventions for influencing team outcomes come from designing the team well in the first place[3]. This all makes sense in theory, but how practical is it?
Mark Mortensen[4] says:

> The dynamism, competitiveness, and scope of work forces organisations to utilize teams with boundaries that are fluid, overlapping, and often disagreed upon.
>
> Mortensen (2015)

Simon Cavicchia and Dorothee Stoffels also question whether the notion of a team having clear boundaries is always appropriate today when the environment is so complex, dynamic, and unpredictable[5]. The team through this lens is viewed only as a mental construct. Boundaries are not objectively real; rather they are socially constructed[6] and different people will have different mental models as to who is in a team and who isn't. Mortensen suggested that up to 25% of a team's membership disagree upon its composition at any point in time[7], a number that resonates with my own personal experience working with teams. I pretty much always ask team members individually who is on the team, before we start working together. It's rare that everyone agrees. And if you ask people outside the team, who is on the team, you find even more variability. I recently asked 14 stakeholders to name every person on their senior leadership team. One person got it right. This may be because there are people in the team who are more junior than their team peers, who are then assumed not to be a fully-fledged member of the team. Or it may be that people belong to more than one team, and people associate them most strongly with another of those teams. Or it may be that people have recently joined, left, or re-joined a team, and people have lost track. Added to all that, as teams progress through their different tasks, and as different people are required to achieve those tasks, and as the world moves ever faster, stability of membership may not be a desirable thing. It may get in the way of having the best people available to tackle the task at hand. It may lead to a team missing important cues in the environment. It may lead to a lack of adaptability and diversity of thought.

Ruth Wageman and colleagues acknowledged that the traditional notion of a team may now be outmoded[8]. To address this, they suggested substituting role stability for membership stability, so that team roles are regarded as stable and bounded even if the role holders come and go. But this frame still values stability when stability is not always a good thing. It just switches the locus of stability from person to role, when it may be that new skills and therefore new roles are required at a particular point in time.

Mortensen suggests that today's organisations increasingly mirror the dynamism of today's economies. To respond to constant change requires us to be nimble, which in turn requires us to decentralise authority, and to become more dynamic and flexible in the way we allocate resource. Through this lens there will be times when not everyone is sure of even an effective team's membership, and when different people hold different perspectives as to the team's boundaries. And people will inevitably belong to more than one team at a time as their expertise is required by multiple stakeholders such that these boundaries increasingly overlap. He suggests that the type of collaboration now required for teams to achieve their goals results in:

- People frequently entering and leaving the team in response to the shifting needs of the team.
- Boundaries between teams overlapping, as many people find themselves working on more than one team at a time.
- Different people holding different perspectives as to who is on the team.

Whilst acknowledging that Wageman's ideas are popular and have been widely cited, Mortensen poses several questions, among them:

What if we defined teams in terms of objectives and not people? In other words, the team, at any given point in time, is the group of people who need to be together to work to a common purpose. This perspective shifts us away from a position where we expect to see clear boundaries and stable member-ship, to a place where we might expect to see quite the opposite – a fluid and dynamic gathering of people shifting and changing in response to the needs of the moment.

What if we viewed teams as part of a system instead of standalone entities? Reflecting on this question may have us realise that team boundaries are not in any sense real – rather they are mental constructs that people may or may not share. This perspective may direct our attention to working with the broader social system or at least recognising that the people we are working with are part of a broader system, and that the small system we call 'team' may not always be the most useful focal point.

What if we considered teams as snapshots in a social process rather than structures? Through this lens, the 'team' is something fleeting and who I might most usefully be working with at any point of time may change just as quickly.

Where you stand in this debate will likely depend on your values and your experience. If you value logic, stability, and structure, then you may lean more toward the traditional perspectives on team. Or if most of the clients you work with seem to value clear boundaries and stability of membership, then again you may lean toward the traditional perspective. If, on the other hand, you do a lot of work in professional services, where teams are brought together to work on a specific client on a specific task, and where certain people are required only at certain stages of a project, you may find Mortensen's questions more interest-ing. Or perhaps you have a contingency model in mind, where you adapt your approach to your perception of the industry, or organisation. Or you may like aspects of both approaches and come up with your own perspective on how it is most helpful to think about a team.

2. What does a team coach do – broad scope?

Not everyone agrees on the broad scope of the team coach. If we consider the life of a team from beginning to end it includes all the work that takes place before a team is formed, as well as what happens once the team has been formed. To what extent does the work that takes place before a team is formed fall under the remit of the team coach?

Traditional team effectiveness models talk about input, process, and outcomes (Figure 3.1)[9]. Inputs describe factors that enable or constrain the functioning of a team, once formed. That would include the organisational context, the formation of a team, and the characteristics of the individuals who come to be a member of the

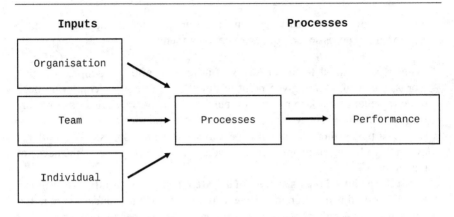

Figure 3.1 Traditional IPO models (after John Mathieu & colleagues, 2008)

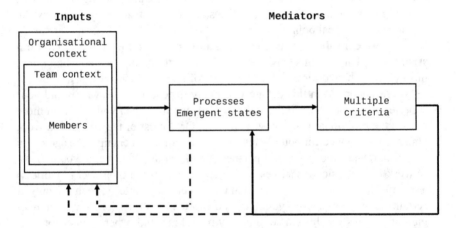

Figure 3.2 IMO models (after John Mathieu & colleagues, 2008)

team. Processes describe the nature of interactions between team members, clearly a focus for the team coach, and outcomes include performance and the personal impact of the team's work on team members.

These IPO models then evolved into Input–Mediator–Outcome–Input models (Figure 3.2)[10] that better reflect the dynamic and cyclical nature of team functioning. They acknowledge, for example, that the work of the team has an impact on the organisational context and the characteristics of individuals, and that outcomes impact the work of the team. Successful outcomes, for example, may lead to the team feeling more energised and cohesive.

These are models of team effectiveness and different authors see the role of the team coach as relatively broad or narrow within those boundaries.

In *The Practitioner's Handbook of Team Coaching*, Colm Murphy and Melissa Sayer[11] say:

> Recognised team inputs, such as the team task, team composition and team size are often already in place and non-negotiable by the time a team coach starts to work with a team. Hence we do not propose to explore inputs too deeply.
>
> Murphy and Sayer (2019)

This is consistent with a perspective that says team coaches work only with intact teams, and implies that team coaches don't get involved in, nor need to know much about task formulation and team composition. Compare that to a different perspective in the same book, this time from Ruth Wageman and Krister Lowe:

> It is important … to make a distinction between team coaching that supports the ongoing process and task work of a team after it is designed and launched from a broader view of team coaching that involves supporting leaders and teams in their effective design, launch, and ongoing internal coaching. Many team coaches support leaders, teams, and organizations throughout all three of these phases.
>
> Wageman and Lowe (2019)

The broad scope of the team coach therefore, is open to debate. Wageman and Lowe claim that interventions focussed on getting the basic design of a team right count for 60% of the variance in team outcomes. They suggest that the initial team launch counts for 30% of the variance, leaving only 10% for hands-on team coaching.

Jacqueline Peters also takes a broad perspective on team coaching[12]. She describes a 'High Performance Team Coaching System' comprising six phases. Two of those phases are 'Coaching for Team Design' and 'Team Launch'. Coaching for Team Design is the second phase of the system and takes place after an initial 'Assessment'. If the assessment reveals any structural issues that might get in the way of a team operating effectively, then the coach is encouraged to work with the team leader individually to address those structural issues, including attracting new talent and performance managing existing talent. The team launch is characterised as a one to three-day facilitated process in which the team coach acts part facilitator, part consultant, and part coach.

The question then for all of us, do we see team recruitment and the launch of the team as being part of our remit as a team coach? Or do we leave that work to others? Or do we potentially cover the whole remit, but make it clear to people we are wearing different 'hats' at different stages of the process? And if we do contribute to the process of selecting a team, how does that impact on our supposed 'neutrality' once the team has been formed? And what do we think about this idea of a team launch? How relevant is the notion of a lengthy facilitated event to launch a team if we see a team as being an ever-changing, dynamic, fluid entity? Lots of questions.

3. What does a team coach do – specific role?

Once we have invented an idea like 'team coaching' then people move quickly to differentiate it from other, related, disciplines. In the team coaching space these efforts doubled down once industry associations began to build competency frameworks and accreditation processes. You can't accredit someone as a team coach without first being clear what team coaching is and identifying the skills and competencies a prospective team coach needs.

Rebecca Jones and colleagues suggest we must be able to differentiate team coaching from other interventions, otherwise we can't develop team coaching theories and the literature is unlikely to evolve. We can't tell whether team coaching works if we haven't distinguished it from other ways of working. And we need to differentiate it in order to sell team coaching, otherwise organisations won't know what they're buying[13]. Others present similar arguments. That rather leaves open the question as to why we need to develop a team coaching-specific literature, or why we need to be able to market team coaching vs a broader focus on team effectiveness.

David Clutterbuck and colleagues also believe we need to differentiate team coaching from other interventions. They compare team coaching to team building and team facilitation in some detail[14]. Team coaching, they suggest, is about improving performance, while team building is about creating greater levels of engagement and trust, and team facilitation is about improving team collaboration. The process of team coaching is dialogic, while team building is activity-based, and team facilitation is about a focus on process, task, and content. Team coaching and team facilitation typically involve multiple interactions, while team building is usually a one-off intervention. This very neat set of distinctions is problematic.

First, these distinctions reflect a particular set of mental constructs, mental constructs unlikely to be shared by everybody. Would all team coaches agree, for example, that if they are helping a team build higher levels of trust, then they are not coaching the team, they are building the team? Would all team builders agree that they are coaching the team when they are engaged in a dialogue pertaining to the team task, and not team building? Would all team facilitators and team coaches agree that they are not facilitating or coaching if they have been engaged to work with the team for a single session?

Scott Tannenbaum and Eduardo Salas write about team effectiveness rather than team coaching and they assign the following roles to the consultant, not the team coach: finding out the real reason why teams may be struggling, helping teams to adapt and self-adjust, helping teams build shared cognitions, helping employees become better team members, promoting the development of psychological safety, etc.[15] People can try, if they think it's useful, to ring-fence team coaching from other forms of intervention, but the client isn't going to be any less confused if other interventionists don't share the same mental models. Other interventionists will still be describing some of the supposed functions of a team coach as falling into their domains.

Second, if we do commit to such a taxonomy, we inevitably have to start talking about different hats. Alexander Caillet and Amy Yeager, for example, suggest that there exist at least five different ways of working with a team, including team facilitation, training, building, consulting, and coaching[16]. They similarly attempt to draw boundaries between these five modalities, in terms of: approach, role, outcomes, and performance impact. A team coach approaches real-time interventions during regular team meetings and work sessions. He/she shares in-the-moment observations and questions leading to immediate improvements in awareness, skills, and effectiveness. The team coach is not there to provide guidance as to the deployment of a method, process, or tool, or to ask the team to engage in learning exercises, or to provide any assessment/advice or exercises in service of learning. Each of the five modalities is useful and all five may be incorporated into a single team engagement, or even a single team event. The more modalities you master, the greater your capacity to be helpful. The document even has a picture of a team practitioner wearing five different hats.

Clutterbuck and colleagues say something quite similar. They say that:

> There is an understanding that the team coach may move between aspects of team coaching, team building, and team facilitation, demanding an enhanced degree of flexibility in their knowledge and skills set.
>
> Clutterbuck et al. (2019)

This makes logical sense, but do we really want to be wearing all these hats? Caillet and Yeager say that it's important the team practitioner educates their clients about the distinctions between these different modalities and what each can achieve, so they know what to contract for. That would require a lot of explicit hat swapping.

This perspective seems to imply that team coaching is not, by itself, a particularly meaningful activity, not if most assignments demand some or most of the other modalities. It requires the coach to be constantly thinking about what hat they are wearing and to be contracting with the client accordingly. This seems very complicated, almost certainly confusing, since there exist multiple versions of team coach vs facilitator vs consultant etc., and even perhaps a waste of time and energy. I have worked with many clients who, frankly, couldn't care less what I call myself, so long as I can help them. Would it not be simpler to define team coaching in broader terms, a definition that potentially includes all the other activities?

Another one for you to decide, of course. You are currently free to define your own personal approach to team coaching *and* to contract as to what you do and don't do (e.g. I am a team coach who doesn't do facilitation). On reflection, do you think it is helpful to try and distinguish between all these different team modalities? And if you do, how will you be clear with yourself and with others what activity you are engaged in at any one time? And if you don't like these taxonomies, how will you contract with your client as to your scope of work?

4. How directive can a team coach be?

Perhaps not at all. David Clutterbuck and colleagues say that a team coach adopts a non-directive, exploratory approach[17]. As we have seen already, Alexander Caillet and Amy Yeager say that a team coach shares observations and asks questions[18] in contrast to other forms of team intervention that entail providing guidance as to the use of a tool, engaging in exercises, or providing any assessment or advice.

In apparent contrast, Alison Hodge and David Clutterbuck suggest that an important aspect of the team coach's role is to educate the team. In the aforementioned study in which I interviewed 36 practising team coaches, 12 of them said that one of their roles was to bring new theory and insights to the teams with which they worked[19]. Most authors position learning as an important element of team development and many, though not all, writers ascribe an educational role to the team coach[20]. Christine Thornton is an exception, suggesting that skills development is more the realm of training[21].

The notion that coaches only observe and ask questions has been questioned in the individual coaching literature, never mind the team coaching literature. Michael Cavanagh questions what he calls overly simplistic client-centric approaches that assume the solution lies within the client[22]. The coach's role, according to this mantra, is only to facilitate the client's discovery of what already exists within. Ask – don't tell. But often the solution doesn't lie within the client, in which case, Cavanagh suggests, it is OK to educate your client, share mental models, and tell them things.

If you believe that to be the case in individual coaching, then it is surely true of team coaching, given that few clients have an in-depth understanding of systems theories, team dynamics, and so on. This is not to suggest that the team coach *doesn't* ask questions and *doesn't* invite the client to make their own sense of the world, and the models and frameworks they may choose to share, but it is to lean away from the idea that the *only* thing the coach does is to ask questions. Cavanagh suggests it may be more helpful to see the creation of solutions as relational, as an emergent property of the interaction between coach and client.

Are we then making a distinction between being directive and being educational? One might make the distinction between telling a team what they *should* do, and telling a team what they *could* do, but this distinction may be less clear in practice than it seems on paper. If, for example, I truly believe that a particular set of actions will help the team move on, does this conviction not sometimes leak out? And if my client asks me what I think, and reveres my perspective so much that I know they will do whatever I suggest, is this not in effect directive?

Where then do you stand on the matter? Do you see a clear distinction between being a team coach and being an educator? Or do you see education and/or advice giving as a fundamental part of your role, such that you will quite happily stand in and suggest/offer advice if and when that seems to be appropriate?

5. What about team dynamics?

Some writers emphasise the role of the team coach in facilitating an improvement in the quality of interpersonal relationships between team members.

Christine Thornton, for example, differentiates between individual coaching and group coaching on the basis that group coaches must have acknowledge of group dynamics[23]. Group analysis:

> Pays particular attention to the relationship between each individual and the group as a whole.
>
> Thornton (2016)

Contrast this to Richard Hackman and Ruth Wageman's theory of team coaching[24], in which they say that:

> The pervasive emphasis on interpersonal processes in the team performance reflects a logical fallacy about the roles of these processes in shaping perform-ance outcomes.
>
> Hackman and Wagemen (2005)

The logical fallacy, according to Hackman and Wageman, is an inference that poor interpersonal relationships cause performance problems, when in fact it is poor performance that causes poor interpersonal relationships. If the latter is true, so the logic goes, then we are wasting our time trying to mend poor relationships because those relationships will remain poor, despite our best efforts, until we shift our efforts to improving performance. Remaining focussed on relationship may be "*quite engaging*" but won't reliably improve team performance. Instead, the coach should focus on team effort, strategy, knowledge, and skill.

This is an interesting debate, though the majority of team coaches seem to lean more toward the view that team dynamics matter, and that the team coach should have an understanding of team dynamics and a capacity to work with those dynamics. Simon Cavicchia and Dorothee Stoffels suggest that many difficulties and obstacles to team performance are only visible at the task level and are unlikely to be addressed by the team coach unless they have some understanding of under-lying dynamics[25]. Hackman and Wageman's assertions have also been challenged in terms of the strength of the underpinning research[26]. But even if that is your per-spective, that team dynamics matter, where do team dynamics sit in your approach to the work? Do you like to start with team dynamics because you agree that if a team has good dynamics it will be better able to achieve its goals? Or do you like to move quickly to clarifying purpose, goals, and clear roles, whilst all the time keep-ing an eye on team dynamics, in the belief that clear purpose and goals will make the work on team dynamics easier? Or do you like to work with both in parallel, in the belief that they are co-contingent? Where do team dynamics sit as part of your overall approach?

6. What does it mean to be a systemic team coach?
There has been much written about systems in the coaching domain. A cursory inspection of LinkedIn reveals the existence of lots of systemic coaches. What

people mean by systemic however, is often left unexplained, which is important because there exist a multitude of systems theories, representing quite different perspectives as to how organisations-as-systems work[27] and different ways of thinking about the work we do.

Many coaches, upon being asked what constitutes being 'systemic', talk in general terms about adopting a holistic perspective, a view from the balcony where the coach can see what's happening outside the team as well as what's happening inside the team. This very general perspective leaves open what sense they are making of what they see from their lofty perspective. Other coaches articulate quite specific definitions as to what they mean by 'systemic' without alerting the reader to the existence of other, equally valid, systemic perspectives. The term 'Systemic Team Coaching' has even been trademarked, Peter Hawkins defining it as a process

> "by which a team coach works with a whole team, both when they are together and apart. The aim is to improve their collaboration, collective performance, stakeholder engagement, collective learnings and increase the value they co-create with and for all their stakeholders"[28].

Driven by a personal desire to better understand the world of systems thinking, I spent a couple of years familiarising myself with systems theories[29,30,31]. Much influenced by Ralph Stacey[32], I identified five broad categories of systems theories, each of which can quite appropriately called 'systemic', and each of which would be expected to elicit different perspectives from the balcony view, and different approaches to coaching a team. Those five categories are

Linear systemic

von Bertalanffy (1969) described general systems theory (GST)[33]. GST is underpinned by three underlying assumptions. First, a social system is a real system. Second, the way systems operate is logical and can be mathematically modelled. Third, an external observer (e.g. a leader, or a coach) can stand outside the system and objectively diagnose how it works.

Some of those systems may be simple, others more complicated. A hot water system is a relatively simple linear system, in which a thermostat detects the temperature of the water and sends signals to a heating element to switch on (if the water is cold) or switch off (if the water is too hot). The linear way of making sense of the world is commonplace. In observing the way that managers make decisions, we often see a search for linear cause and effect, for the right levers to pull.

Some team coaches think in linear fashion. The coach who sees the team as an intact system that can be diagnosed objectively from the outside, for example. Such a coach probably privileges hierarchy as an important means by which the team operates, and therefore privileges the role of the leader. Comparing the team to a simple system, the coach tends to focus on one, maybe two, aspects of the team's functioning and believes that by improving that aspect of functioning, the effectiveness of the team as a whole will be improved. For example, the team coach who believes that improving team dynamics will improve performance, or the coach who believes clear goals and roles will inevitably lead to enhanced team effectiveness. Simon Cavicchia and Dorothee Stoffels suggest that a leaning toward the use of psychometrics, and simple models such as the Lencioni model, may all represent a leaning toward a more linear philosophy[34].

This perspective, and the actions the coach takes consequently, may sometimes be effective, but sometimes not.

Non-linear systemic

Peter Senge and colleagues (1990) listed five disciplines required of a learning organisation, the fifth of which was 'systems thinking'[35]. Through this lens the observer is advised to watch out for less obvious cause and effect relationships, relationships that are distanced in time and/or space, and for circles of causality and positive feedback loops. The three underlying assumptions underpinning GST still apply, but the relationships between system components of the system are not assumed to be simple or linear.

A systemic team coach looking through this lens would still think in terms of being able to stand aside from the team and diagnose its functioning objectively. The coach would still see hierarchy as an important mechanism by which the team operates. But the coach would be on the lookout for other factors influencing the functioning of the team and would expect the functioning of some of those factors to be quite complicated and difficult to discern. The coach may still focus on one or two aspects of team performance but doesn't expect outcomes to be wholly predictable because the 'system' is complicated. The system may be better compared to an aircraft engine, or a laptop (my laptop anyway), or the human body.

Collaborative systemic

Gregory Bateson suggested that people are not able to perceive reality directly, that people can only ever experience a personal representation of reality[36,37]. Accordingly, Peter Checkland and colleagues said that attempts to mathematically model the functioning of systems will often fail, because the world is too "complex, problematical and mysterious" for humans to understand[38]. So, whilst an organisation may function as a system, the essential nature of the system is too complex to observe directly. This challenges the second assumption underpinning GST, that the operation of a social system can be modelled mathematically. This perspective recognises that different people have different perspectives on a situation, and that people need to come together to build a working model of the system together. The co-constructed model is more likely to approximate reality than anyone's individual perspective[39,40,41].

This approach still implies that the leader or coach can stand outside a system and diagnose its functioning, but that the leader or coach is likely to ask others to accompany them on the journey, and to be genuinely curious as to what those others are seeing and thinking.

A team coach working through this lens may still place great value on the outcome of a team diagnostic but will be open as to what the results signify. This coach encourages team members to share perspectives and to be open to different points of view. He/she is inevitably interested in the dynamics of the team, since the extent to which the team can understand and integrate the perspectives of others will depend upon the quality of communication between team members. This coach is also likely to be more flexible in terms of the scope of the work, being less attached to their own perspective of events, and more curious as to what others think.

Complex systemic

Theories of complex adaptive systems (CAS) recognise that people are not passive entities and their behaviours are unpredictable. People make sense of events together, in their local environments. From broader interactions between these different coalitions emerge aggregate behaviours. Local sub-systems are subject to feedback from the broader system and respond accordingly. Interaction at the local level continues to evolve as people continue to make sense of events, whilst seeking to survive in the broader system.

This is a fundamentally different perspective on organisation-as-system. Through this lens, the leader or coach cannot meaningfully regard their diagnosis as to what's going on in a team as anything more than the outcome of a local interaction. The leader and coach are fooling themselves if they think they can stand outside the team, assess its functioning, then design an intervention based on that 'objective' perspective. Through this lens both leader and coach are intrinsic components of the system, whether they like it or not. The leader cannot control outcomes, since you cannot control how people make meaning, nor oversee everything everyone does, but the leader can effectively engage and influence.

A team coach working through this lens recognises that perceptions of team membership, common objectives, team roles, etc., are all in a state of constant flux. The coach encourages the team to become more aware of the nature of its functioning, and of the impact that conversations outside the team have on conversations taking place inside the team. The team is encouraged to understand how goals, objectives, and intentions emerge, and to focus on its capacity to influence those conversations.

Meta-systemic thinking

These complexity theories tend to depict the organisation as one big system with numerous sub-systems and sub-sub-systems. But organisations are not systems in any meaningful sense and nor are teams. An organisation is a mental construct. We all have a perspective as to who is in an organisation and who is not, but our perspectives are different. Do we include people on short-term contracts? Do we include the person who sits with our team but is employed by a joint-venture partner? Do we include the barista in the downstairs café, who everyone talks to? And in making those decisions, are we then assuming that those who we imagine to be outside the 'organisation' are less influential in their interactions? To compare an organisation to a system may be helpful. As George E.P. Box expressed it, "All models are wrong, but some are useful"[42]. Sometimes though, the metaphor is less useful.

One drawback of the team-as-organisation and organisation-as-system metaphors is that we risk over privileging interactions between people within the boundaries of that 'system'. For example, in seeking to understand the dynamics of a team, if I over-privilege the personalities, values, and beliefs of the people in the room, I may under-privilege the influence of people outside the room, and the conversations taking place between those people and members of a team.

A team coach looking at the world through a meta-systemic lens may still think systemically but recognises the limitations of those metaphors and recognises when they may be useful and when not. This coach will likely meet their clients where they are and be prepared to engage with their clients through their way of making meaning, but the questions they ask will inevitably come from a meta-perspective, those questions carefully considered in service of being most helpful.

Through this lens you, and every coach, are systemic. The question is – what kind of systemic are you?

7. How big should a team be?

David Clutterbuck writes that team coaches shouldn't work with teams if they are too big because if they are too big then it becomes hard for the team to gel, and you will see dynamics emerge, such as social loafing, which will get in the way of performance[43]. This perspective is born of a long literature on team size, that suggests the ideal size for a team is somewhere between four and eight people[44].

It makes sense for all sorts of practical reasons to limit the size of a team. In traditional teams the leader is asked to spend time with each team member individually, setting objectives, discussing performance and career goals. The bigger the team, the less likely these conversations are to be high quality, or to happen at all. And it takes time to engage a big group of people in any kind of meaningful conversation and team dynamics become exponentially more complex. Some coaches, therefore, won't work with much bigger teams. Instead, they advise the team leader to make the team smaller first. Georgina Woudstra, for example, suggests that if a team has more than eight members the team is unlikely to be effective[45]. Lucy Widdowson and Paul Barbour agree that larger teams are more difficult to work with but say also that they have worked with teams comprising more than 25 team members and suggest ways of managing the larger numbers[46], including designing structures that have people moving in and out of small groups.

The small-team perspective is linked to perspectives more broadly on teams. If I believe in the importance of clear boundaries and stable membership, and the idea that everyone on a team is focussed on achieving the same outcomes, then I may encourage the team to talk about everything, together, as often as possible. I've come across teams some of whose members complain that they get left out of certain conversations. Being left out is interpreted as being a secondary team member whose value is not wholly recognised. Through a different lens we may recognise that a 'team' faces many issues, many of those issues arising unexpectedly and requiring a swift response. If we hold to the adage that members of a team have a common purpose, then it doesn't make sense that everyone on the team needs to be present to address every issue the team faces. Some issues require the attention of lots of people, some issues require the attention of a much smaller group of people. Holding that as a principle may create a different meaning for people who find themselves invited to some discussions and not others. Limiting team numbers to eight or nine may not make so much sense through this lens. What if we view the team as a temporary mental construct and we know we will require the commitment of 15 people to address a particular topic?

So, what is your philosophy on team size, and how does this show up in the conversations you have with clients as to the kind of work you will and won't do, and how you choose to engage with larger teams?

8. When is the best time to coach a team?
Team development models postulate what stages a team might go through in its lifetime providing insights as to what work the team might most usefully engage in, depending what stage it is at. The best-known model is the Tuckman Model[47,48,49].

In the *Forming* stage of the model the group orients to its task, establishes ground rules, and team members establish relationships with each other and others outside the team. In the *Storming* stage group conflict emerges. Team members resist being pulled into group structure and assert their individuality. In the *Norming* stage people come to accept each other's differences. New norms are established and people discover how best to work with each other. In the *Performing* stage team members become more adaptable in service of achieving their goals, prepared to shift roles in service of the greater good. The final *Adjourning* stage was added twelve years after the original article was published.

The Tuckman Model is used by very many team coaches and implicitly assumes that coach and team should meet and work on a regular basis. The decision point is rather how to use that session time, depending on where the team is at in its development. If the team is at the *Forming* stage, for example, it may be most useful to chart out the stakeholder groups with whom the team needs to build relationships. If the team is at the *Storming* stage, for example, it may be most useful to work on emotional management, in service of helping people express themselves most effectively, etc. The Tuckman Model has been much challenged, notably with reference to its origins in working with small therapy groups. Nevertheless, the model remains popular and is still used by team coaches, many of whom equate a group's preparedness to meet on a regular basis with its commitment to the process and its likelihood of being successful.

Connie Gersick critiqued the Tuckman Model[50,51]. She noted that the Tuckman Model, and most other models besides, are essentially linear, charting the team's progress through a linear pathway, that has to be experienced stage-by-stage with none of those stages being skipped. She said also that the model implies a closed system, in which the group progresses solely in terms of the conversations that take place between team members. Gersick came up with a quite different model, based initially on her work with eight project teams. She found that her teams were inert for long periods, sticking to their approach to the task regardless. These teams reviewed their approach to the work only at three points in their life. At the beginning of the task they decided very quickly how they would work together, typically at their first meeting together. They would then stick with this approach until the midpoint of their time together, when they dropped old patterns, re-engaged with supervisors, and adopted new perspectives on their work. This process happened quickly and preceded another long stage of inertia. Finally, at the end of their time together, the group engaged in a reflective process as the life of the team neared an end. Gersick called this process 'punctuated equilibrium'.

Why, we might ask, would a team be prepared only to review its functioning halfway through its life? Gersick suggests:

> Halfway is a natural milestone, since teams have the same amount of time remaining as they have already used, and they can readily calibrate their progress. Adult development research offers analogous findings. At midlife, people shift their focus from how much time has passed to how much time is left. Levinson found a major transition at midlife, characterized by 'a heightened awareness of mortality and a desire to use the remaining time more wisely'.
>
> Gersick (1988)

Of course, not all teams are project teams with pre-determined end points, but Hackman and Wageman[52] suggest that Gersick's findings can nevertheless be generalised to other teams because all teams know when they are about halfway finished, based on their consumption of available resources or their progression to a goal, for example. The authors relate Gersick's findings explicitly to team coaching, suggesting that coaches focus on a team's readiness for coaching based on where they are in their life cycle. Team coaching will be most effective when it meets the needs of the team at the stage it's at, needs that are relatively predictable viewed through the lens of the model. Looking through the lens of the model implies also that coaching may be irrelevant or ineffectual during the great majority of a team's time together – the two long periods of inertia. Teams may be quite resistant to working with a coach during these periods of inertia, a lack of readiness that need not imply a lack of commitment to coaching, or to the goals of the team, nor a lack of ability on the part of the coach.

Many people think these team development models are helpful, if not essential, but Simon Cavicchia and Dorothee Stoffels suggest that all such models may tempt us into thinking too linearly[53]. These models imply that teams progress from stage to stage in a sequence of steps, and this includes the Gersick Model with its presumption that teams have limited, predictable, life spans. The linear perspective may overlook the complex and ever-changing nature of the environment, and of the dynamics within a team. If demands on a team suddenly intensify, then the team dynamic is likely to respond accordingly. If membership of the team is fluid and changeable, the idea that there is some underlying process of team development may not be so helpful.

Again, in contemplating these debates, we don't need to choose one perspective or another. There exist various perspectives on team development and patterns of working. What does your experience tell you about how you can be most useful to a team, in what way, and when? Is it helpful to think about that last session you had with a team, that didn't go very well, and frame it with reference to a team development process, rather than question the team's commitment and/or your competence? Or are such models too simplistic?

9. Is it OK for people to belong to multiple teams?
What do you think and say if members of a team repeatedly fail to show up for team coaching sessions because they are busy elsewhere? What does it say about their commitment or lack of commitment to the team's cause? Jim Shore and Shane Warden[54] clearly believe that people should belong to only one team. They wrote:

> Some organizations like to assign people to multiple teams simultaneously. If your company practises this fractional assignment, I have some good news. You can instantly improve productivity by reassigning people to one project at a time.
>
> Shore and Warden (2007)

Few organisations seem to have taken this advice. Mark Mortensen reports that up to 95% of people work in more than one team at the same time[55].

Some writers suggest that belonging to a few teams may improve performance. Working for several teams at once enables:

• More connections
• More opportunities to learn
• A greater range of experiences

And there are disadvantages:

• Excessive demands on individual's time, leading to health and wellbeing issues
• Lack of time to build connections more widely
• Feeling peripheral and/or disconnected to some teams
• No time to learn

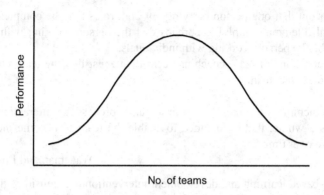

Figure 3.3 General relationship between number of teams and performance

There then exists a bell-curve relationship between the performance of the individual and how many teams they are a member of (Figure 3.3). Multi-team membership may have an adverse impact on the team's focus, its learning, performance, and wellbeing over time[56] *and* it can lift productivity and encourage knowledge sharing[57,58,59].
The literature doesn't suggest an ideal number of teams to be a part of, because that number will depend on multiple factors, including task complexity, individual commitment to specific roles in different teams, the propensity of team leaders to collaborate effectively, the ability of team members to build and maintain relationships, their levels of technical expertise etc.

So, the literature is somewhat divided. Some writers say organisations work better when people belong to one team and one team only, others encourage people to participate in several teams, with suggestions as to how to make this work best[60]. What is your perspective?

10. Can I coach the team and individuals on the team at the same time?
David Clutterbuck and colleagues say:

> We can say with some confidence that team coaching is not coaching individual members of a team separately, because this does not involve collective dialogue.
>
> Clutterbuck et al. (2019)

Somewhat confusingly they also say:

> However, a team intervention may well include both individual and collective coaching.
>
> Clutterbuck et al. (2019)

They point out that one person carrying out both roles may be complex and present ethical dilemmas, implying perhaps that the person working with the team shouldn't be the person working with individuals.

Some definitions of team coaching seem to suggest that the team coach work only with the intact team:

> Team coaching is an intervention in a team's process, an interaction with the team as a whole, that is intended to enable the team to become increasingly effective over time.
>
> Wageman and Lowe (2019)

> A team-based learning and development intervention that considers the team to be a system and is applied collectively to the team as a whole.
>
> Jones, Napiersky, and Lyubovnikova (2019)

> An interaction between a coach and a team, in order to reflect upon, define and implement new strategies to achieve team purposes.
>
> Dimas, Rebelo, and Lourenco (2016)

Some team coaches think carefully before engaging with individuals on a team, while simultaneously working with the team as a whole. People being coached individually may be worried that what is disclosed in the individual coaching session may be revealed, perhaps inadvertently, in a team session. People not being coached individually may be concerned that the team coach has stronger relationships and greater loyalty toward those being coached individually. Those with individual access to the team coach may lean toward presenting their thoughts and

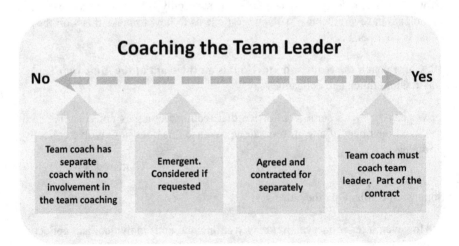

Figure 3.4 Perspectives on coaching team leader and team simultaneously (Gill Graves, 2021)

concerns to the coach in the hope that the coach will pass on their concerns to the team leader without them having to voice those concerns themselves. There are lots of issues for the team coach to consider.

So then, are you happy to work with team members individually while working with the team as a whole? Gill Graves spoke to ten team coaches[65,66]. She found some who said they wouldn't work with individuals, including the team leader, and others who said they worked with the team leader individually all the time, that this was an essential part of the process. And some whose approach sat somewhere in the middle (Figure 3.4).

Do you sit at one end of the spectrum, or somewhere in the middle? If in the middle, do you have guidelines that you refer to in responding to individual requests for coaching? And if you are happy to work with individual team members, how do you manage that process?

The wise team coach

In reviewing this material on debates, it becomes clear that different people hold different perspectives on different issues. If our personal approach to team coaching is to be robust, then we need to challenge what we are told, not in an effort to dismiss or disrespect, but in service of our own learning. In this section I'll share with you how I went about further seeking to understand what various authors meant when they talked about the value of coaching systemically.

I found the following quotation helpful to guide me through the process. Writing about the systems thinking community nearly thirty years ago David Lane and Mike Jackson criticised the use of the phrase 'systems thinking'[67]:

> The majority of system dynamicists are in the USA and, prompted by Peter Senge's book [The Fifth Discipline] they had started calling their single subject 'systems thinking'. From the European perspective this usage was bewildering, or looked rather arrogant, or just seemed ignorant of the wide range of techniques that shelter beneath the expansive umbrella of that term.
>
> Lane and Jackson (1995)

They further warned that:

> Usage of the term 'systems thinking' is spreading in the SD (systems dynamics) community with an enthusiasm which verges on the hegemonic. The employment of this term to describe our own single methodology is virtually to deny the existence of any other, if we use that term for our own discipline, we are putting ourselves in a mental prison.
>
> Lane and Jackson (1995)

Hegemonic means ruling or dominant (I had to look it up).

We might usefully consider these statements with respect to what is happening in the team coaching domain today. Several authors have attempted to define 'systemic coaching' or 'systemic team coaching' on behalf of us all, some even trade-marking the term, but there exist many different systems theories and therefore many different systemic perspectives on team coaching.

In reading various texts on 'systemic coaching' I found only a few that articulated in any detail their underlying philosophy. Christine Thornton, for example, says her approach to team coaching is underpinned by systems theory, specifying chaos and complexity theory[68]. She characterises systems theory in terms of relationships rather than things, on noticing patterns of change rather than static snapshots. She says that teams are social systems or subsystems and talks about nested systems. The team coach, she says, needs to locate the boundary of the team where it is most usefully drawn, rather than that boundary being objectively placed. She refers to the self-organising characteristic of complex systems.

Thornton's rejection of more mechanistic ways of thinking about the system suggests her approach is not linear systemic. The focus on looking for subtle relationships between cause and effect suggest her theory may be to an extent non-linear systemic, whilst acknowledging the team coach has choice in deciding where to locate boundaries sounds like collaborative systemic. She refers explicitly to aspects of chaos theory and complex adaptive systems. She asserts categorically that teams are systems, which seems to rule out the meta-systemic perspective.

This analysis helps me compare my thinking to hers. If my own perspective is also complex systemic, I may be more likely drawn to exploring her thoughts. If the complex systemic perspective doesn't appeal then I may decide to read it anyway, in order to further explore, or I may just close the book and seek out something different.

Peter Hawkins earlier descriptions of systemic team coaching appear to include elements of linear/non-linear thinking, in that the team coach is counselled not to "become caught up in the team culture or dynamic", advice that implies the team coach is able to stand aside from the dynamics of others in the room and observe events objectively[69]. His later book, written with Eve Turner[70] appears to eschew linear/non-linear thinking in favour of perhaps the collaborative systemic. They say:

> … you can never know something, let alone somebody, objectively … your perception of them happens through the lenses of your own rich and sense subjectivity.

Hawkins and Turner (2020)

Hawkins' 2017 description of team coaching appears to reflect a shift toward a complexity perspective in that he writes about the need to focus on the dynamic relationship between the team and its environment[71]. His 2019 book builds on this theme, encouraging the coach to focus on the relationships between entities rather than the entities themselves[72]. Hawkins and Turner emphasise the changeability of goals whose evolution can only be understood through dialogue with stakeholders. All of these factors point to the further emergence of a complex systemic perspective. Hawkins' 2017 positioning of ecosystemic team coaching as distinct from systemic team coaching is less clear. Ecosystemic team coaching appears to be different in that it explicitly acknowledges the ecology as well as communities and culture, but this difference appears to be a matter of scope rather than underlying philosophy.

Sean O'Connor and Michael Cavanagh also depict the organisational system in terms of systems and sub-systems[73]. The smallest system is the cell, followed by the organ, person, dyad, team, corporation, industry, etc. They suggest that the internal dynamics of individuals are not the focal point for team coaching. The team coach is most interested in the conversations between team members and the relationship between the team and its wider environment. They suggest that 'fractal patterns' can be discerned in coaching, a concept intrinsic to complexity theories.

Simon Cavicchia and Dorothee Stoffels write about relational systemic coaching[74]. They compare and contrast their approach to more linear perspectives, suggesting that the role of the team coach is to help the team discover things for themselves rather than provide theories, models, and tools. The linear perspective over-privileges the supposition of clear team boundaries and under-privileges the influence of relationship. Their model points to the unpredictable and ever-changing nature of relationship. They list six premises of relational systemic coaching:

1. Individuals and teams are embedded in a web of relationships and have a system around them.
2. A focus on different levels of a system, including individual, team, and wider organisational system.
3. All behaviour is a form of communication.
4. Human beings make meaning in conversations.
5. Difference provides information.
6. The effective team coach is curious and reflexive and indifferent to predetermined outcomes.

This perspective seems quite similar to that of O'Connor and Cavanagh in that it embraces many of the ideas from theories of complex adaptive systems, while retaining the notion of systems and sub-systems, which a meta-perspective would perhaps hold more lightly.

These authors all provide some clarity as to the philosophies underpinning their notions of systemic. Other authors are less explicit. Nevertheless, any theory can be examined in an attempt to understand the underlying systemic philosophy. Hackman and Wageman's theory of team coaching[75], for example, would appear to be based largely on linear thinking. They suggest that team effectiveness is a function of three processes: i) group effort, ii) the appropriateness of performance strategies, and iii) team member knowledge and skill. Focusing on the quality of relationships between team members, they say, is less useful, because performance often seems to drive interpersonal relationships rather than the other way around. The suggestion that team performance is a function of three processes and three processes only, and the selective citing of evidence pointing to the relative ineffectiveness of working with team dynamics, suggest that the authors are looking for a simple and straightforward model by which they can explain team performance.

You may not much like this particular perspective on systems and that's fine. But prod, poke, and challenge. Don't always rely on the author telling you their findings are based on research or that 'everyone agrees' to a particular perspective. The quality of your 3Ps will depend on the extent to which you leverage your powers of critical thinking.

Next

Now we have reviewed some of the debates around team coaching, I invite you to continue your journey in defining your own approach to team coaching. I will share 'ten cool ideas' you may find worthy of inclusion in your *philosophy*. I will share with you what 51 other team coaches had to say about their *purpose* in doing the work. And I will share with you insights on translating philosophy and purpose into *practice*.

But before we set off on that journey, let me first share with you where I think the three biggest industry associations appear to sit with regard to these debates. In other words, let's attempt to explore these apparently objective competency models in service of revealing the more subjective philosophy that sits beneath.

References

1. Wageman, R. & Lowe, K. (2019). Designing, Launching, and Coaching Teams: The 60-30-10 Rule and its Implications for Team Coaching. In: D. Clutterbuck, J. Gannon, S. Hayes, I. Iordanou, K. Lowe & D. Mackie (Eds.), *The Practitioner's Handbook of Team Coaching*. Routledge.
2. Hackman, J.R. & Katz, N. (2010). Group Behavior and Performance. In S.T. Fiske, D.T. Gilbert & G. Lindzey (Eds.), *Handbook of Social Psychology*. John Wiley & Sons.
3. Wageman, R. & Lowe, K. (2019). Designing, Launching, and Coaching Teams: The 60-30-10 Rule and its Implications for Team Coaching. In: D. Clutterbuck, J. Gannon, S. Hayes, I. Iordanou, K. Lowe & D. Mackie (Eds.), *The Practitioner's Handbook of Team Coaching*. Routledge.
4. Mortensen, M. (2015). *Boundary multiplicity: Rethinking teams and boundedness in the light of today's collaborative environment.* INSEAD Working Papers No. 2015/31/OBH. Retrieved from https://papers.ssrn.com/sol3/papers
5. Cavicchia, S. & Stoffels, D. (2024). The Future of Team Coaching. In: E. De Haan & D. Stoffels (Eds.), *Relational Team Coaching*. Routledge.
6. Barley, S.R. & Kunda, G. (2001). Bringing Work Back In. *Organization Science, 12(1)*, 76–95.

7. Mortensen, M. (2015). *Boundary multiplicity: Rethinking teams and boundedness in the light of today's collaborative environment.* INSEAD Working Papers No. 2015/31/OBH. Retrieved from https://papers.ssrn.com/sol3/papers

8. Wageman, R., Gardner, H., & Mortensen, M. (2012). The Changing Ecology of Teams: New Directions for Team's Research. *Journal of Organizational Behavior, 33*, 301–315.

9. Mathieu, J.E., Travis Maynard, M., Rapp, T., & Gilson, L. (2008). Team Effectiveness 1997–2007: A Review of Recent Advancements and a Glimpse into the Future. *Journal of Management, 34(3)*, 410–476.

10. Mathieu, J.E., Travis Maynard, M., Rapp, T., & Gilson, L. (2008). Team Effectiveness 1997–2007: A Review of Recent Advancements and a Glimpse into the Future. *Journal of Management, 34(3)*, 410–476.

11. Murphy, C. & Sayer, M. (2019). Standing on the Shoulders of the Science of Team Effectiveness: Building Rigour into Your Team Coaching Design. In: D. Clutterbuck, J. Gannon, S. Hayes, I. Iordanou, K. Lowe & D. Mackie (Eds.), *The Practitioner's Handbook of Team Coaching.* Routledge.

12. Peters, J. (2019). High Performance Team Coaching: An Evidence-Based System to Enable Team Effectiveness. In: D. Clutterbuck, J. Gannon, S. Hayes, I. Iordanou, K. Lowe & D. Mackie (Eds.), *The Practitioner's Handbook of Team Coaching.* Routledge.

13. Jones, R.J., Napiersky, U., & Lyubovnikova, J. (2019). Conceptualizing the Distinctiveness of Team Coaching. *Journal of Managerial Psychology, 34(2)*, 62–78.

14. Clutterbuck, D., Gannon, J., Hayes, S., Iordanou, I., Lowe, K., & Mackie, D. (2019). Introduction: Defining and Differentiating Team Coaching from Other Forms of Team Intervention. In: D. Clutterbuck, J. Gannon, S. Hayes, I. Iordanou, K. Lowe & D. Mackie (Eds.), *The Practitioner's Handbook of Team Coaching.* Routledge.

15. Tannenbaum, S. & Salas, E. (2021). *Teams That Work. The Seven Drivers of Team Effectiveness.* Oxford.

16. Caillet, A. & Yeager, A. (2018). *Introduction to Corentus Team Coaching.* Corentus.

17. Clutterbuck, D., Gannon, J., Hayes, S., Iordanou, I., Lowe, K., & Mackie, D. (2019). Introduction: Defining and Differentiating Team Coaching from Other Forms of Team Intervention. In: D. Clutterbuck, J. Gannon, S. Hayes, I. Iordanou, K. Lowe & D. Mackie (Eds.), *The Practitioner's Handbook of Team Coaching.* Routledge.

18. Caillet, A. & Yeager, A. (2018). *Introduction to Corentus Team Coaching.* Corentus.

19. Lawrence, P. & Whyte, A. (2017). What do Experienced Team Coaches do? Current Practice in Australia and New Zealand. *International Journal of Evidence Based Coaching and Mentoring, 15(1)*, 94–113.

20. Farmer, S. (2015). Making Sense of Team Coaching. *The Coaching Psychologist, 11(2)*, 72–80.

21. Thornton, C. (2016). *Group and Team Coaching: The Secret Life of Groups, 2nd edition.* Routledge.

22. Cavanagh, M. (2006). Coaching from a Systemic Perspective: A Complex Adaptive Conversation. In: D.R. Stober & A.M. Grant (Eds.), *Evidence Based Coaching Handbook.* John Wiley & Sons.

23. Thornton, C. (2016). *Group and Team Coaching. The Secret Life of Groups, 2nd edition.* Routledge.

24. Hackman, J.R. & Wageman, R. (2005). A Theory of Team Coaching. *The Academy of Management Review, 30(2)*, 269–287.

25. Cavicchia, S. & Stoffels, D. (2024). Why Relational? In: E. De Haan & D. Stoffels (Eds.), *Relational Team Coaching*. Routledge.
26. Hastings, R. & Pennington, W. (2019). Team Coaching: A Thematic Analysis of Methods Used by External Coaches in a Work Domain. *International Journal of Evidence Based Coaching and Mentoring, 17(2)*, 174–188.
27. Lawrence, P. (2021). Team Coaching: Systemic Perspectives and their Limitations. *Philosophy of Coaching: An International Journal, 6(1)*, 52–82.
28. Hawkins, P. & Turner, E. (2020). *Systemic Coaching. Delivering Value Beyond the Individual*. Routledge.
29. Lawrence, P. (2021). *Coaching Systemically. Five Ways of Thinking About Systems*. Routledge.
30. Lawrence, P. (2021). Team Coaching: Systemic Perspectives and their Limitations. *Philosophy of Coaching: An International Journal, 6(1)*, 52–82.
31. Lawrence, P. & Skinner, S. (2023). *The Wise Leader. A Practical Guide for Thinking Differently About Leadership*. Routledge.
32. Stacey, R. (2012). *Tools and Techniques of Leadership and Management. Meeting the Challenge of Complexity*. Routledge.
33. Bertalanffy, L. von. (1968). *General Systems Theory*. George Braziller.
34. Cavicchia, S. & Stoffels, D. (2024). Why Relational? In: E. De Haan & D. Stoffels (Eds.), *Relational Team Coaching*. Routledge.
35. Senge, P. (1990). *The Fifth Discipline*. Random House.
36. Hawkins, P. (2004). A Centennial Tribute to Gregory Bateson 1904–1980 and His Influence on the Fields of Organizational Development and Action Research. *Action Research, 2(4)*, 409–423.
37. Kobayashi, V.N. (1988). The Self-Reflexive Mind: The Life's Work of Gregory Bateson. *Qualitative Studies in Education, 1(4)*, 347–359.
38. Checkland, P. (2000). Soft Systems Methodology: A Thirty-Year Retrospective. *Systems Research and Behavioral Science, 17*, S11–S58.
39. Atkinson, C.J. & Checkland, P. (1988). Extending the Metaphor "System". *Human Relations, 10*, 709–725.
40. Checkland, P. (2012). Four Conditions for Serious Systems. *Systems Research and Behavioral Science, 29*, 465–469.
41. Checkland, P. & Haynes, M. (1994). Varieties of Systems Thinking: The Case of Soft Systems Methodology. *Systems Dynamics Review, 2/3*, 189–197.
42. Box, G.E.P. (1976). Science and statistics. *Journal of the American Statistical Association, 71(356)*, 791–799.
43. Clutterbuck, D. (2015). Wave the Red Flag. *Coaching at Work, 10(3)*, 18.
44. Woudstra, G. (2021). *Mastering the Art of Team Coaching*. Team Coaching Studio Press.
45. Woudstra, G. (2021). *Mastering the Art of Team Coaching*. Team Coaching Studio Press.
46. Widdowson, L. & Barbour, P.J. (2021). *Building Top Performing Teams. A Practical Guide to Team Coaching to Improve Collaboration and Drive Organizational Success*. Kogan Page.
47. Tuckman, B.W. (1965). Developmental Sequence in Small Groups. *Psychological Bulletin, 63(6)*, 384–399.

48. Tuckman, B.W. & Jensen, M.A. (1977). Stages of Small-group Development Revisited. *Group Organisational Studies, 2(4)*, 19–27.
49. Bonebright, D.A. (2010). 40 years of Storming: A Historical Review of Tuckman's Model of Small Group Development. *Human Resource Development International, 13(1)*, 111–120.
50. Gersick, C.J.G. (1988). Time and Transition in Work Teams: Toward a New Model of Group Development. *Academy of Management Journal, 31(1)*, 9–41.
51. Gersick, C.J.G. (1989). Marking time: Predictable Transitions in Task Groups. *Academy of Management Journal, 32(2)*, 274–309.
52. Hackman, J.R. & Wageman, R. (2005). A Theory of Team Coaching. *The Academy of Management Review, 30(2)*, 269–287.
53. Cavicchia, S. & Stoffels, D. (2024). Why Relational? In: E. De Haan & D. Stoffels (Eds.), *Relational Team Coaching*. Routledge.
54. Shore, J. & Warden, S. (2007). *Art of Agile Development*. O'Reilly Media.
55. Mortensen, M. (2015). *Boundary multiplicity: Rethinking teams and boundedness in the light of today's collaborative environment*. INSEAD Working Papers No. 2015/31/ OBH. Retrieved from https://papers.ssrn.com/sol3/papers
56. Margolis (2020). Multiple Team Membership: An Integrative Review. *Small Group Research, 51(1)*, 48–86.
57. Margolis (2020). Multiple Team Membership: An Integrative Review. *Small Group Research, 51(1)*, 48–86.
58. Wimmer, J., Backmann, J., & Hoegl, M. (2019). In or Out? Exploring the Inconsistency and Permeability of Team Boundaries. *Small Group Research, 50(6)*, 699–727.
59. O'Leary, M.B., Mortensen, M., & Woolley, A.W. (2011). Multiple Team Membership: A Theoretical Model of its Effects on Productivity and Learning for Individuals and Teams. *Academy of Management Review, 36*, 461–478.
60. Lawrence, P. (2023). *The Team Leader Instruction Manual*. Longueville Media.
61. Clutterbuck, D., Gannon, J., Hayes, S., Iordanou, I., Lowe, K., & Mackie, D. (2019). Introduction: Defining and Differentiating Team Coaching from Other Forms of Team Intervention. In: D. Clutterbuck, J. Gannon, S. Hayes, I. Iordanou, K. Lowe & D. Mackie (Eds.), *The Practitioner's Handbook of Team Coaching*. Routledge.
62. Wageman, R. & Lowe, K. (2019). Designing, Launching, and Coaching Teams: The 60-30-10 Rule and its Implications for Team Coaching. In: D. Clutterbuck, J. Gannon, S. Hayes, I. Iordanou, K. Lowe & D. Mackie (Eds.), *The Practitioner's Handbook of Team Coaching*. Routledge.
63. Jones, R., Napiersky, U., & Lyubovnikova, J. (2019). Conceptualizing the Distinctiveness of Team Coaching. *Journal of Managerial Psychology, 34(2)*, 62–78.
64. Dimas, I., Rebelo, T.M., & Lourenco, P. (2016). Team Coaching: One More Clue for Fostering Team Effectiveness. *European Review of Applied Psychology, 66(5)*, 233–242.
65. Graves, G. (2021). What Do the Experiences of Team Coaches Tell Us About the Essential Elements of Team Coaching? *International Journal of Evidence Based Coaching and Mentoring, S15*, 229–245.
66. Graves, G. (2024). *Team Coaching with Impact at Work*. Rethink.
67. Lane, D.C. & Jackson, M.C. (1995). Only Connect! An Annotated Bibliography Reflecting the Breadth and Diversity of Systems Thinking. *Systems Research, 12(3)*, 217–228.

68. Thornton, C. (2016). *Group and Team Coaching: The Secret Life of Groups, 2nd edition*. Routledge.
69. Hawkins, P. (2011). *Leadership Team Coaching: Developing Collective Transformational Leadership*. Kogan Page.
70. Hawkins, P. & Turner, E. (2020). *Systemic Coaching. Delivering Value Beyond the Individual*. Routledge.
71. Hawkins, P. (2017). *Leadership Team Coaching: Developing Collective Transformational Leadership, 3rd edition*. Kogan Page.
72. Hawkins, P. (2019). Systemic Team Coaching. In: D. Clutterbuck, J. Gannon, S. Hayes, I. Iordanou, K. Lowe & D. Mackie (Eds.), *The Practitioner's Handbook of Team Coaching*. Routledge.
73. O'Connor, S. & Cavanagh, M. (2016). Group and Team Coaching. In: T.Bachkirova, G. Spence & D. Drake. *The SAGE Handbook of Coaching*. SAGE.
74. Cavicchia, S. & Stoffels, D. (2024). Why Relational? In: E. De Haan, E. & D. Stoffels, D. (Eds.), *Relational Team Coaching*. Routledge.
75. Hackman, J.R. & Wageman, R. (2005). A Theory of Team Coaching. *The Academy of Management Review, 30(2)*, 269–287.

Chapter 4

Ten debates and three global industry associations

In Chapter One I considered the limitations of characterising something as complex as team coaching solely in terms of skills and competencies. Yet some industry associations may do just that, the rationale being that we must present a united face to the world and ensure we are all providing the same, consistent, quality service. In this chapter I'll attempt to characterise each of the three biggest industry association's team coaching competencies (or equivalent) with reference to the ten debates outlined in the last chapter, and then reflect on what the analysis is telling us.

In Figure 4.1 I present my *interpretation* of where each of the industry associations appear to sit on each of the ten debates framed in Chapter Three as indicated by their competencies/performance indicators. These are my interpretations only and may not wholly reflect the intentions of their architects.

The ICF integrate their coaching competencies into their pre-existing eight coaching competencies designed for individuals. The EMCC website refers to 12 core standards and 125 performance indicators[1]. The performance indicators are positioned differently to competencies in that they represent guidelines as to what an evaluator might see rather than hard and fast rules. The Association for Coaching has 11 team coaching competencies[2]. What do they all have in common and how are they different?

1. What is a team?

The ICF comes down firmly on the side of a team being something real and boundaried. Competency 1 *(demonstrates ethical practice)* says that the team coach coaches the client team as a single entity, and competency 4 *(cultivates trust and safety)* says that the team coach should promote the team viewing itself as a single entity with a common identity.

In contrast, the EMCC performance indicators (PI) don't ask the team coach to ensure the team regards itself as a single entity. It may however be inferred that the team is assumed to be relatively stable. PI 5 says that the team coach should develop

DOI: 10.4324/9781003546108-5

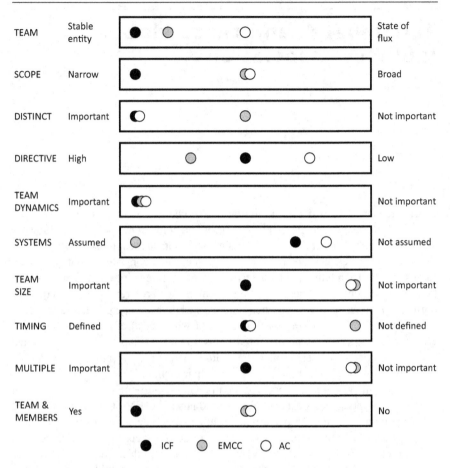

Figure 4.1 Where three global industry associations appear to stand with regard to the ten debates

a planned and structured approach to the team coaching intervention, which will be hard if the composition of a team is fluid and dynamic. There is a strong emphasis on the use of initial diagnostics, the value of which is arguably diminished working with a team whose membership is constantly changing.

The AC competencies place less emphasis on planning and structure than do the EMCC PIs. There is an explicit requirement that the team coach re-designs their approach as the needs of the team change in competency 2 (*establishes the coaching agreement*), and a requirement that the coach works flexibly to meet the team's changing needs in competency 7 (*live team coaching*). There is perhaps an inference that the membership of a team is stable in the reference to a somewhat linear consulting model in competency 10 (*team knowledge*).

2.   What does a team coach do – broad scope?

The ICF competencies imply that the coach's scope is narrow, in that they say that the client is always the team, and not the team leader. This is highlighted in a video accompanying the competencies[3]. If the client is the team and not the team leader, this implies that the team coach's work begins only when the team is formed. Neither the EMCC PIs nor AC competencies say that the team coach should think more narrowly or more broadly about their scope, though there is no explicit mention to bringing the team together or launching the team.

3.   What does a team coach do – specific role?

The ICF competencies position team coaching as something quite distinct from other forms of team intervention. Competency 1 says that the team coach maintains the distinction between team coaching, team building, team training, team consulting, team mentoring, team facilitation, and other team development modalities. Competency 3 (*establishes and maintains agreements*) says that a team coach explains what team coaching is and is not, including how it differs from other team development modalities, and that it is important for the team coach to highlight the difference between team coaching and other team development modalities. The introduction to the team coaching competencies spell this out in more detail.

- *Team building* is defined as a short-term intervention comprising exercises, with a focus on enhancing relationships. It doesn't address team conflict and is delivered by an instructor.
- *Team training* is defined as a short-term intervention based on a curriculum, with a focus on acquiring new skills. It doesn't address team conflict and is delivered by a trainer.
- *Team consulting* is defined as a short-, medium-, or long-term intervention comprising the sharing of expertise, with a focus on generating insights. It doesn't address team conflict and is delivered by a consultant.
- *Team mentoring* is defined as a long-term, staccato, intervention comprising the sharing of knowledge, with a focus on generating insights. It doesn't address team conflict and is delivered by a mentor.
- *Team facilitation* is defined as a short-term intervention comprising facilitated dialogue, with a focus on gaining clarity. It doesn't address team conflict and is delivered by a facilitator.
- *Team coaching* is defined as a long-term intervention comprising some kind of relationship between a team and one or more team coaches, facilitated dialogue, and a focus on achieving goals and team sustainability, delivered by a team.

The AC competencies also say that the team coach should communicate the differences between team coaching and other team interventions (e.g. team building and facilitation) clearly and transparently. There is less emphasis in the EMCC PIs on clarifying these differences. There is some distinction between team coaching and team facilitation, however, in the description of the eighth core standard, which suggests the effective team coach is aware of the benefits of partnering with facilitators.

4.   How directive can a team coach be?

The ICF competencies suggest that there are times when the team coach will be directive and times when not. Competency 1 says that the team coach will need to be directive more often than the individual coach, when being directive will help the team understand their growth areas and the nature of the team coaching process.

The EMCC PIs make no explicit reference as to whether the team coach is directive or otherwise. They do however suggest that it is the coach's role to:

- Plan the team coaching assignment, rather than it being a shared responsibility (PI 5).
- Generate an understanding of the system within which the team is operating (PI 31).
- Explain how his/her chosen models work in practice (PI 7).
- Explain the relevance of systems thinking (PI 8).
- Offer hypotheses as to how the system is functioning (PI 64).

Generally, there is a strong focus on systems thinking (see below) and the team coach's role is to make sure the team understands systems thinking principles, specifically those principles associated with complex adaptive systems.

The AC competencies make no explicit reference to whether a team coach should be more or less directive. The team coach is required to design the overall approach, without necessarily having to include the client, and to explain the approach to the client (competency 2). The coach is also required, however, to work to the team's agenda throughout the assignment, rather than an agenda pre-determined by the coach, and to continually seek feedback from the team and other stakeholders in informing the ongoing agenda and intervention design (competency 2). The team coach is required to work flexibly, adapting his/her style and the intervention to the team's changing needs (competency 7). There is no suggestion that the team coach needs to be more directive than the individual coach.

5.   What about team dynamics?

All three industry associations are clear that the team coach needs to understand team dynamics. ICF Competency 2 (*embodies a coaching mindset*) says that team coaches should work with supervisors to ensure that they don't become entangled in team dynamics. The same competency says that the team coach must be aware of, and alert to how team dynamics play out. Competency 6 says that a team coach can enhance team performance by bringing to light individual team member behaviours that may detract from performance. The EMCC PIs also say that the team coach should understand models and thinking on group dynamics, including how those dynamics change when the team is under pressure (PI 35). The coach should raise the client's awareness of those dynamics (PI 63) and help the team understand how its dynamics impact on the success of the team (PI 95). AC competency 6 (*awareness and insight raising*) says that the team coach notices and names interactions, behavioural exchanges, and patterns between team members, and that they share observational feedback with the team. Competency 10 says that the team coach understands and helps a team make sense of its group dynamics.

6.   What does it mean to be a systemic team coach?

The ICF competencies don't use the words 'system' or 'systemic', and so we cannot say that the coach is being explicitly nudged toward a particular way of thinking about systems. I do though discern a leaning toward the linear systemic. First, team coaches are required to be objective in all their interactions (competencies 1 and 2). If this means being able to stand aside from proceedings and view what's happening without being influenced by others, then this feels quite linear in contrast to a collaborative systemic perspective, for example, which acknowledges how we are all wholly subjective in how we make sense of what we notice.

Second, the ICF competencies say that the coach should be completely honest in all his/her dealings with the team and must bring all conflict to the surface (competency 1). If this means the coach sharing every thought or perspective with the team in-the-moment, then this again seems to lean towards a linear perspective along the lines of being transparent is a 'good' thing and always likely to lead to good outcomes. But many of the coaches I know think carefully as to when and how they bring conflict to the surface. They are forever asking themselves – based on my perspective of this team dynamic, what is the most useful thing to do right now? They don't believe it is always useful to share every observation, nor do they believe that the conditions are always right for surfacing conflict. They pay attention to the team dynamic, and their role within that team dynamic, in a way that is more akin to complex systemic ways of thinking.

Third, the ICF competencies suggest that the coach should encourage participation and contribution by all team members (competency 4). Again, this seems to assume that full participation by everybody is required for a team to be most effective. Constantly speaking out is seen as a good thing, which feels like quite a western assumption, perhaps because so many of the coaches involved in the design of the ICF competencies were from Europe and the US. These mantras may discourage the coach from helping the team understand how it functions, exploring how that functioning may be helping and hindering the team's performance. That may or may not be asking quieter people to speak up more.

Fourth, the ICF competencies suggest that a coach should ensure that communication from individual members of the team is directed to the team and should redirect communication within the team when it is directed to the coach (competency 4). The coach should enter into the dialogue only as necessary to enhance team process and performance (competency 5 – *maintains presence*). This may be a useful rule of thumb but doesn't appear to lend itself to a process of exploration whereby the team (including the coach) explore how they are currently functioning and how they might usefully focus differently.

In contrast to the ICF competencies, the EMCC PIs make frequent reference to systems (PIs 11, 31, 39, 59, 65, 66, 68, 69, 70, 72, 73, 80, 87, 97, 99, 100, 102, 104, 107, 100, and 111). Two of these references define what is meant by systems thinking. PI 80 says that the team coach engages in professional supervision to help develop his/her developing awareness of complex adaptive systems, and PI 87 says the team coach works to develop the resilience required to work in a complex adaptive system.

AC competency 9 (*working with the organisational system*) says that the team coach must understand the wider system in which the team operates, must use language appropriate for the team and organisation, work within the organisation's values and policies, align team coaching goals to support broader organisational aims, understand the relationship between key stakeholders and the wider ecosystem, encourage connectivity between the team and the organisational system, and demonstrate an understanding of power dynamics. There is no reference to specific systems theories, indeed competency 10 directs the coach to become aware of systems theories (plural) and makes no specific mention of, for example, theories of complex adaptive systems.

7. How big should a team be?

None of the industry associations make direct mention of team size. The ICF competencies imply a limited team size given that everyone's voice should be heard.

8. When is the right time to coach a team?

The ICF competencies are not explicit about timing, though in the introduction they do say that a team coach works with a team over a period of months and contrast team coaching with team mentoring where the mentor relationship with the team is described as staccato. Does that imply the team coach relationship is more even and regular? The EMCC PIs say nothing about timing. The AC competencies say that team coaches understand (and therefore presumably apply) models of maturity and lifespan development (competency 10), suggesting the coach is expected to modify their approach to whatever the perceived stage of development may be.

9. Is it OK to coach teams with part-time members?

The ICF competencies make no direct comment on whether it is acceptable for people to belong to more than one team, though it may be inferred people shouldn't belong to too many teams, given the coach's role in encouraging the team to view itself as a single entity with a common identity. Neither the EMCC nor the AC say whether it's OK or not for people to belong to multiple teams.

10.   Can I coach the team and individuals on the whole team at the same time?

The ICF competencies suggest that the team coach *should* be coaching individuals as well as the team as a whole. Competency 1 says that the coach should make sure conversations with individuals remain confidential. Competency 3 refers to private discussions with individual team members, and competency 5 says that the team coach should be present for the team as a whole *and* for each individual. The EMCC PIs have less to say. PI 4 says that the coach specifically gathers information from the team leader, which implies at least one conversation with the team leader individually, and consistently refers to the team and team leader separately. AC competency 3 (*establishes a safe and trust-based relationship with the client*) says that the team coach may have relationship with team members aside from his/her relationship with the team leader, and that the team coach attends to individual team member's needs during the coaching assignment.

This is how the three competency/performance indicator frameworks compare with reference to the ten debates. I chose these ten debates because they stood out to me in reviewing the literature, but we can of course compare the frameworks on other dimensions too. They differ in terms of defining the client, for example. Whilst the ICF states clearly that the client is the team and not the team leader, the EMCC PIs say that the coach should apply contracting principles with the team leader, at least initially and the AC competencies leave the definition of client open (competency 2). The EMCC PIs say that the team coach should develop and implement a team diagnostic, while the ICF and AC don't oblige the coach to use such diagnostics, though they refer to them. All three frameworks mention the potential value of working in tandem with another team coach, but the EMCC PIs place most emphasis on co-coaching. They have an entire core standard on co-coaching, perhaps leaning more heavily toward co-coaching as a norm.

What to make of it?

The three frameworks have lots in common. There is a tendency to think of the team as a stable entity. There is a tendency to distinguish team coaching from at least team facilitation, if not other forms of intervention as well. All three models say that the team coach needs a good understanding of team dynamics. None of them suggest that the team coach cannot work with individual team members as well as with the whole team, at least on occasion.

And there are differences. The ICF model is very clear that the team is the client, not the team leader and is particularly specific on differentiating team coaching from other forms of intervention. The EMCC model is full of references to systems and systems thinking, specifically theories of complex adaptive systems, and it comes across (to me) as being quite directive in that domain. The AC model is probably the least directive model and the least deterministic and precise as to what a team coach should do.

If these models were each to claim they were the best, then we would have an issue. In fact, the EMCC are quick to say that their framework is new and that it remains a working document. The AC are also keen to point out that the discipline of team coaching is still developing, and their framework will require ongoing review[4]. The ICF, by contrast imply that their framework will require updating only in five to seven years and represents a 'gold standard'[5]. Regardless of how often these frameworks are updated we shouldn't be surprised if they remain distinct, not once we understand how they came to be.

All three of the associations point to how much work went into building their competencies. The EMCC framework took two years to develop and included consultation with practitioners and 'thought-leaders' and a survey of more than 500 respondents. The AC process took a similar length of time, and the ICF process took 16 months. What did this hard work entail?

The ICF refer to their process as being research-based. We need to understand though what they mean by 'research'. Their process was based largely on a literature research and job analysis. They make specific reference to a paper by Lucy Widdowson and colleagues[6]. That paper was a piece of meta-research, a study of 115 research articles, conducted by a team of 17 team coaching 'experts'. The authors reviewed the literature and looked for common themes. In looking at team coaching competencies, for example, they reviewed the work of Grijalva and colleagues[7], Peter Hawkins[8], Leary-Joyce and Lines[9], John Mathieu and colleagues[10], Carr and Peters[11], Christine Thornton[12], and many others, and used David Drake's mastery model[13] as a scaffold to create a team coaching competencies framework. Notice then that this paper summarises a portfolio of informed perspectives. There is no direct analysis of the relationship between competencies and outcomes – because few such studies exist. Jacqueline Peters and Catherine Carr found 17 academic studies, only five of which studied the impact of the work of an external professional coach. The paper is, in essence, a summary of various people's practical judgments. We must question the value of attempting to distil one single model out of all these perspectives. First, the aggregated perspective may miss important aspects of some individual perspectives. Second, aggregating different practices with different underpinning philosophies may result in something less coherent, not more coherent. Third, there may be no need to aggregate – all the different individual perspectives may be equally impactful.

Turning now to job analysis, this methodology involves talking to practitioners. Since team coaching is so new, the best way to define it is to ask those people who currently call themselves team coaches what it is they do[14]. The ICF process comprised a series of workshops and surveys, with a primary focus on North America and Europe. This sounds like a very rigorous process but is subject to the Tatiana Bachkirova and Carmelina Lawton Smith critique that what coaches have done in the past is not necessarily what coaches ought to be doing in the future[15]. Furthermore, if most of the coaches interviewed are from a single coaching association, then that association's underlying philosophy and beliefs are likely to predominate.

None of the associations in their accreditation programs directly evaluate their coaches to see if they are exercising each of the competencies. The ICF process consists of training, experience, and passing a knowledge exam. The ICF website provides five sample questions from the knowledge exam that each reflect a quite definite view as to what a team coach should do[16].

It may sound like I am seeking to diminish these models. I am not. What I am trying to do is illustrate how each of these models reflects a collective approach to team coaching. None of them can demonstrate that deploying their competencies will lead to better outcomes. They represent three different collective practical judgments, each of them of course different, because different people came together to share experiences. Again, there is no evidence that a single collective approach is more effective than any of the individual approaches that informed the research, so we cannot relate to any of these frameworks, or any framework yet to be written, as a definitive single best way of coaching teams. We ought nevertheless to regard all these frameworks as interesting and useful. The wise coach doesn't seek to diminish all the hard work that has gone into producing these frameworks. The wise coach is curious to understand these frameworks, how they were constructed, and what lessons there are to be learned in informing his/her own practice.

The construction of a global competencies framework, through this lens, represents the construction of one giant set of 3Ps. Each framework is based on a collective set of theories, frameworks, experiences, and values; those of the participants and of the industry association. They reflect the collective purpose of participants and association, and they reflect a collective perspective on what good team coaches actually do. The global coaching associations are not the only groups of people discussing what constitutes good team coaching then publishing their findings for others to read. Andrew Day and Dorothee Stoffels offer their Team Coaching Skills Model[17]; Georgina Woudstra describes the Team Coaching Wheel[18]; Gill Graves details the PiE Team Coaching Model[19]; Alexander Caillet and Amy Yeager write about the Corentus Team Coaching Model[20], etc. All of these models are based on some form of evidence.

Your personal approach to team coaching is just as valid as all these collective approaches. You can conduct literature reviews too if you want. You can interrogate not only your personal experiences, but you can listen to other team coaches talking about their experiences in supervision groups, podcasts, and webinars. You can read books. Your approach is as good as anyone else's, and it is also a collective approach in that everyone you listen to and speak to will play a role in influencing your 3Ps.

In the meantime, do not assume that the team coaching world will soon align around a single approach. Andrew May suggests that our thinking in this space may be more likely to fragment further, as people coalesce around philosophical and professional differences[21]. Tammy Tawadros suggests that schools of thought may polarise with linear approaches to team coaching at one end, and more dialogic, relational, and systemic approaches at the other end[22]. That doesn't mean we should all look to take a position and defend it. So again, don't dismiss these competency models, just see them for what they are, and be curious about them and learn from them.

References

1. www.emccglobal.org/accreditation/itca/
2. www.associationforcoaching.com/page/TeamCoachingAccreditation
3. https://coachingfederation.org/credentials-and-standards/team-coaching/competencies
4. www.associationforcoaching.com/page/team-coaching-podcast-series-team-coaching-accreditation
5. https://coachingfederation.org/credentials-and-standards/team-coaching/competencies
6. Widdowson, L., Rochester, L., Barbour, P., & Hullinger, A.M. (2020). Bridging the Team Coaching Competency Gap: A Review of the Literature. *International Journal of Evidence Based Coaching and Mentoring, 18(2)*, 35–50.
7. Grijalva, E., Maynes, T.D., & Badura, K.L. (2020). Examining the "I" in team: A Longitudinal Investigation of the Influence of Team Narcissism Composition on Team Outcomes in the NBA. *Academy of Management Journal, 63(1)*, 7–33.
8. Hawkins, P. (2017). *Leadership Team Coaching: Developing Collective Transformational Leadership, 3rd edition*. Kogan Page.
9. Leary-Joyce, J. & Lines, H. (2018). *Systemic Team Coaching*. AOEC Press.
10. Mathieu, J., Maynard, M.T., Rapp, T., & Gilson, L. (2008). Team Effectiveness 1997–2007: A Review of Recent Advancements and a Glimpse into the Future. *Journal of Management, 34(3)*, 410–476.
11. Carr, C. & Peters, J. (2013). The Experience of Team Coaching: A Dual Case Study. *International Coaching Psychology Review, 8(1)*, 80–98.
12. Thornton, C. (2016). *Group and Team Coaching: The Secret Life of Groups, 2nd edition*. Routledge.
13. Drake, D.B. (2009). Evidence is a Verb: A Relational Approach to Knowledge and Mastery in Coaching. *International Journal of Evidence Based Coaching and Mentoring, 7(1)*, 1–12.
14. Jones, R.J., Napiersky, U., & Lyubovnikova, J. (2019). Conceptualizing the Distinctiveness of Team Coaching. *Journal of Managerial Psychology, 34(2)*, 62–78.
15. Bachkirova, T. & Lawton Smith, C. (2015). From Competencies to Capabilities in the Assessment and Accreditation of Coaches. *International Journal of Evidence Based Coaching and Mentoring, 13(2)*, 123–140.
16. https://coachingfederation.org/credentials-and-standards/team-coaching/exam
17. Day, A. & Stoffels, D. (2024). Working at Relational Depth: Skills in Relational Team Coaching. In: E. De Haan & D. Stoffels (Eds.), *Relational Team Coaching*. Routledge.

18. Woudstra, G. (2021). *Mastering the Art of Team Coaching*. Team Coaching Studio Press.
19. Graves, G. (2024). *Team Coaching With Impact at Work*. Rethink.
20. Caillet, A. & Yeager, A. (2018). *Introduction to Corentus Team Coaching*. Corentus.
21. De Haan, E., Stoffels, D., Cavicchia, S., Knights, A., Day, A., Bell, J., Sills, C., Tawadros, T., Stubbings, A., Birch, D., & Hanley-Browne, R. (2024). The Future of Team Coaching. In: E. De Haan & D. Stoffels (Eds.), *Relational Team Coaching*. Routledge.
22. De Haan, E., Stoffels, D., Cavicchia, S., Knights, A., Day, A., Bell, J., Sills, C., Tawadros, T., Stubbings, A., Birch, D., & Hanley-Browne, R. (2024). The Future of Team Coaching. In: E. De Haan & D. Stoffels (Eds.), *Relational Team Coaching*. Routledge.

Chapter 5

The 3Ps – philosophy

In Chapter Two you started to think about your 3Ps and in Chapter Three I shared just some of the debates taking place within the team coaching industry. In Chapter Four I had a look at where I sense the big three global industry associations stand on those debates.

For me the biggest insight from Chapter Four is that whilst there are similarities between the three industry frameworks, there are also differences. Each model is the outcome of lots of work, including literature reviews and structured interviews with experienced practitioners, yet they are all different. Their models are of course influenced by theory, but they are also informed by the values and experiences of the people they spoke to and each organisation's collective values and experiences. Each of these organisations has a somewhat different approach to competencies, some quite specific as to how team coaches should behave, others leaving more wriggle room. These associations each have their own mission and purpose, whether it be to define generic standards for all, or to encourage people to reflect more for themselves. We can expect these different philosophies to show up in their frameworks. These philosophies are, to an extent, self-perpetuating. Those coaches who like certainty and structure and clear guidelines, may gravitate toward industry associations that appear to reflect those values. Those coaches who see the industry differently, at its best a reflective collective, ever learning and growing, may be drawn to a different association. Whichever association you are most drawn to, all of them have something useful to offer, and none of them are objective nor can offer us a definitive perspective on team coaching.

As most writers on organisational team coaching are keen to point out, we have barely begun to understand some aspects of team coaching. We cannot expect experienced 'expert' practitioners to agree with each other, because they each have their own beliefs and values and are inevitably drawn to different communities. So, we ought to be keen to understand their different approaches and to learn from them, but as wise team coaches we are not going to take any of these models as definitive nor accept their competencies and accreditation processes as categorical. Instead, we are free, in a 'post-professional' industry as some authors have described it[1], to develop our own personal approaches to team coaching. In this chapter I invite you to further explore your underlying philosophy.

DOI: 10.4324/9781003546108-6

In Chapter Two I encouraged you to think about your experiences and values as well as your favourite theories and frameworks.

Experiences

Take the time to think about some of your adventures so far as a team coach. Think about some of the most memorable moments in your time as a team coach so far. What stands out for you? And what did you learn from those experiences?

I recall a recent incident, working with a large team of people. We were near the end of the session, and I asked people to break into smaller groups to reflect on their experience of the session. Of the big team, only two were women and for this exercise they paired up together. When they shared their reflections with the wider group one of the men in the group made a light-hearted comment that could have been construed as reinforcing and enabling or patronizing and condescending. Whatever the intention of the speaker, it landed heavily. One of the men in the group picked up on the comment and questioned whether it was appropriate. Neither of the women wanted to comment further and we moved on. The session finished shortly afterwards, and the two women approached me to let me know how strongly they felt about the comment. They said they felt distanced by their colleague, "*reduced to their sex*". They sought my input into thinking through what they would do next. In reflecting on the incident, by myself, with one of the women, and with my supervisor, I concluded that should such an incident happen again I would play a more active role in managing the conversation. In terms of my philosophy, I needed to rebalance my energies in allowing a team to manage their own dynamics and ensuring the space was safe for everyone. And I needed to dedicate more time to understanding the world from a feminine perspective and to exploring gender and gender dynamics.

We must think more broadly, of course, than just our experiences as a team coach. I have spent a lot of time the last few years exploring systems theories and challenging more linear approaches to managing change and relationships. Why? I believe that interest originates in part from my experiences as a leader. I worked for BP plc, a large multinational, for fourteen years. I joined the company thinking that I was entering a world of logic and rationality. In 1999 I accepted a role working for a brand-new retail business in Japan. In my first role I was responsible for managing the investment case, ensuring the case for investment was always consistent with actual revenues and costs. When I first arrived, we were charged with building a business delivering annual profits of $25m or more. For the first year or so, we were on track. Then, we were told that company strategy had changed. Now we needed to explain how we could become a $50m business. So, we rethought the strategy and came up with a new story. Then, a year or so later, as BP pursued its 'elephant' strategy, we needed to show how we could become a $100m business. We struggled to make a case for becoming a $100m business within the desired time frames and it was decided to sell our business.

The world changes, people change, strategies change, expectations change. What surprised us were the stories told to explain the decision to sell. For two years we were regarded as a great innovation play, doing new things, on the way to becoming a good medium-sized business. But after the decision was made to sell the business two Global Vice Presidents came to Japan to explain why we were being sold. They told the whole company that the retail business was being sold because the business had failed to grow quickly enough and that the original business case had been over-optimistic. As we listened, it started to become clear how the decision had been made, who had been talking to who, how different people's understandings of the original business case and different opinions of each other, had come together to form an overall narrative which didn't resonate with anyone working in the business. This wasn't 'logical'. Different people saw different things and made sense of what they saw differently. People made meaning by talking to other people and from those conversations emerged new narratives, new stories. No one was necessarily being dishonest or Machiavellian. To understand what happened required us all in the business to look beyond the logical and rational to see the world for how it is – a constantly shifting, changing, amalgam of event, fact, and perception. This experience, and other experiences working for the same organisation, shaped my perspective on the world and no doubt stimulated my interest in systems theories and their applicability to leadership.

Which of your experiences in life have played a significant role in determining how you go about your work as a team coach?

Values

Working with more experienced coaches we sometimes find people move quickly to thinking about theories, models, and frameworks, skating over their values and a deeper sense of what is important to them.

I did a self-assessment recently which suggested my top five strengths are:

- Perseverance – finishing what we start and taking pleasure in completing tasks.
- Creativity – thinking of new ways to do things.
- Judgment – thinking things through and examining them from all sides.
- Curiosity – taking an interest in experience for its own sake.
- Love of learning – mastering new skills, topics, and bodies of knowledge.

My 91-year-old mother recently told my 22-year-old daughter that what she most admired about me was my perseverance. I don't generally give up on things. If part of me thinks about stopping or giving up, another part of me expresses itself very critically. Once I'm working with a team then I will stay with that team, even if things are not going well, and I (sometimes unconsciously) expect the members of the teams I work with also to persevere, to work hard to help the team to become more effective. This is useful sometimes. Other times it may get in the way of me stopping to reflect as to whether I/we are on the right path and may make it hard for me to engage with people for whom perseverance is not so important.

I am creative. I enjoy exploring new possibilities and am forever looking for new ways of doing things. This means I connect well with people who are also creative and innovative. It may also mean I may sometimes neglect the tried and trusted and may find it hard to engage with people who expect clearly defined process, procedure, and outcomes. I may become distracted from the ultimate goal by the opportunity to experience something new and different.

I am inclined to talk through issues and explore them from all angles. I am happy to spend time discussing the topic at hand ensuring everyone's views are heard. Sometimes this is helpful, particularly when working with a team which is yearning to make more time to stop and reflect. At other times my approach may frustrate teams, teams who are more action-oriented, keen to move quickly to a solution.

I am curious. In thinking what to do next with a team, I will always lean toward trying something new. Along with curiosity goes a strong love of learning. I am always seeking out new ideas and wondering how those ideas might translate into something useful. This is helpful when working with teams who are similarly curious and keen to learn. It works less well with teams who have little interest in the conceptual and more interest in just getting on with what works and has been shown to work in the past.

I'd encourage you to spend some time thinking about your values and how they inform your approach to team coaching before moving on to the next section. In the next section I'll share with you some 'cool ideas' from the literature on team effectiveness. As you read through these ideas, deciding which are interesting and which are not, you might also usefully reflect on why the ideas you choose sit well with you. Are you looking for completely different ways of thinking, for example? Or are you looking for ideas which offer immediate practical application? Or ideas that will enable you to connect more deeply with your teams, etc.?

Ten cool ideas

Starting with the idea of the meta-team.

1. The meta-team

The first of the ten debates in Chapter Three focussed on how we think about teams. We considered team coaching philosophies that talk to clear boundaries and stable membership, and alternative philosophies based on the notion of a team as something dynamic, fluid, and constantly changing. When teams are constantly changing it's usually because people are constantly moving from team to team, often belonging to more than one team at a time, adding value where their efforts will be most appreciated at any given point in time.

In such circumstances it's often the case that there exists a bigger pool of people from which specific teams are constantly being formed and reformed. Diana

Santistevan and Emanuel Josserand suggest that organisations in which teams are this fluid might usefully think in terms of an intermediate structure that they call the meta-team[2]. They define the role of a meta-team as providing a shared sense of reference that members take into all the contexts in which they work. Jessica Mesmer-Magnus and colleagues came up with a similar notion in writing about 'multiteam systems'[3]. Robert Hirschfeld and colleagues reported that teams whose members have a high level of teamwork knowledge, perform better than teams that don't[4], which supports the idea that enhancing the broader meta-team's capacity to work effectively with others may translate into improved performance at the micro-team level. Scott Tannenbaum and colleagues suggest that employees can usefully be taught 'transportable' teamwork competencies[5]. Rachael Hanley-Browne suggests that the industry as a whole may collectively shift its focus away from the single team and toward enterprise[6].

The notion of meta-teams links to ideas around teaming and shared leadership. Amy Edmondson describes the construction of the Beijing National Aquatics Centre, an innovative and iconic building constructed for the 2008 Olympic Games. Dozens of people contributed to the design of the building, coming to the task in temporary groups of experts[7]. Edmondson names the process by which people worked together as teaming. She talks about the conditions under which teaming may be necessary, for example, when trying to accomplish something that hasn't been done before, such that it's not possible to determine in advance what skills and knowledge may be required, and when. Or when client needs are quickly changing and evolving.

This approach to team development requires everyone to contribute to the process of teaming, rather than rely only on designated leaders. Tripp Driskell and colleagues suggest that good teamers have a low need for hierarchy. They tend to be confident, expressive, and emotionally stable[8]. Amy Edmondson says good teamers speak up. They communicate well and collaborate, they are comfortable taking risks, and they reflect openly with others[9].

Teamers can only effectively team if they are empowered to do so. This requires a particular approach from the team's designated leader. A leader who wants to manage every detail of a project, who wants to sign-off every action, and sees it as their role to ultimately make all decisions, won't get the best out of a team of good teamers. The team leader may have to commit to sharing leadership. Shared leadership is not the same thing as delegation. When leadership is shared, people across the team are directly responsible for, and take accountability for, functions such as building the team, monitoring team performance, stakeholder management, and representing the team in specific forums[10]. To assign these roles is to assign decision-making and accountability. It isn't just about asking people to do all the work before you make the decision.

Emergent leadership is a version of shared leadership in which the leader does not formally allocate shared responsibilities. Instead, people on the team step into leading aspects of the team's functioning without being asked. The leader of the team (and the rest of the team) chooses, consciously or otherwise, to encourage those people to assume those additional accountabilities, or they correct the behaviour of the individual, reining them in. If people find themselves reined in once or twice, it's unlikely they will keep on seeking to take on more work.

I think the idea of meta-teams is a cool idea, and it has already been picked up on by various writers in the team coaching space. For me this idea, as part of my philosophy, leads me to question my purpose. As a team coach, do I continue to focus my efforts on helping individual teams become more successful, or do I want to allocate more energy at the meta-team level, helping people become better teamers and thereby helping multiple teams at once?

2. The dialogic coach

As I've mentioned several times now, a few years ago I interviewed 36 experienced team coaches to find out what they did[11]. Five made specific reference to dialogue, either using dialogue as an explicit framework for coaching or in terms of helping the team to understand the nature of dialogue and to engage in dialogue itself. One coach talked about a team initially perceived by others to be dysfunctional. He said:

> I was referred to work with a group of project managers and used dialogue. I got them to review in turn what they got from their regular meetings. Someone banged their first on their desk after about 20 minutes and said, 'This is rubbish!', but we kept on going round the room, asking each person to talk about what they wanted to get from each other. Another 20 minutes later the same person shouted out 'I've got it!' He was gobsmacked at what he learned from listening to others.
>
> Lawrence and Whyte (2017)

One of David Clutterbuck's earlier definitions of team coaching included explicit reference to dialogue:

> Helping the team improve performance, and the processes by which performance is achieved, through reflection and dialogue[12].
>
> Clutterbuck (2007)

Other writers also make reference to dialogue[13-15], often with reference to the work of David Bohm[16] or William Isaacs[17]. In a contribution to *The Practitioner's Handbook of Team Coaching* seven of us shared a dialogic approach to coaching teams[18]. The model emerged from an experiment, when the seven of us gathered to spend two days in a UK hotel to engage in dialogue about dialogue, with no clear intention as to what would emerge. The model emerged as did a short book, called *The Tao of Dialogue*[19].

The word 'dialogue' requires some consideration. It's like most words in the English language – open to interpretation. Many people think of *dia*logue as *duo*logue, a conversation between two people, not hard to do and not difficult to understand. But the 'dia' in dialogue doesn't mean 'two' – it means 'through', and dialogue is envisaged as a process in which people make meaning of events through their interactions with others. To achieve this requires putting aside our preconceptions, prejudices, and certainties. William Isaacs writes about our 'noble certainties', those certainties and assumptions we hold dear, without necessarily realising the impact of holding those assumptions. In a hierarchy, for example, it may be that there is a general subscription to beliefs such as:

- Making decisions is the role of the leader.
- Leaders get to be leaders because they're better at making decisions than anyone else.
- Leaders are more experienced than their direct reports and have a broader perspective.

And so on. If I hold these assumptions unsuspended, then I am unlikely to consider perspectives that diverge from what I've already decided and I'm unlikely to spend much time talking to people more junior than me. Other common noble certainties include:

- Meetings are a waste of time.
- Gen Z-ers expect to be paid a lot of money for not doing much work.
- People who talk a lot have nothing much to say.
- If you don't look smart – it means you're not serious.
- Old people are wiser than young people.

All of these assumptions limit the extent to which we are prepared to suspend (not dismiss) what we believe in seeking to understand what others are trying to say. Our collective assumptions, as a team, limit the extent to which we can build relationships, trust, and mutual understanding.

Dialogue is also about saying what needs to be said in the moment. In many organisations this voicing component is missing. Amidst uncertainty, people need to know what their leaders are thinking. When leaders say nothing, because they don't have a definitive answer to the questions people are asking, that always heightens anxieties. In the absence of the leadership voice, people make up stories as to what is going on, and those stories are often based on people's worst fears.

In the team there are things that get voiced, and things that don't. Many of the things that don't get voiced, don't get voiced because people are afraid that others will get upset, angry, or take offence. But teams have an intuitive understanding as to the extent to which things get shared, an understanding that sets limits to the team's capacity to truly engage and work together effectively. If we are to express ourselves in a way that encourages engagement and collaboration, we need to express ourselves free of those judgments and noble certainties. We need to think in terms of offering a perspective rather than delivering a mandate. When we offer a perspective, we leave room for the other person to say something different. When we deliver a mandate, we leave no such room. To leave the space for someone else's perspective is to be respectful. If we aren't good at expressing ourselves respectfully, then our perspectives are likely to emerge laced in judgment and prejudice.

If this is what dialogue means, to listen and voice free of preconception, prejudice and certainty, then pure dialogue isn't just hard, it's virtually impossible, because to engage in dialogue requires us to be aware of our preconceptions, prejudices, and certainties, and none of us are 100% self-aware. Nevertheless, we can commit to doing our best, and commit to getting better at it as we become more self-aware.

Dialogue requires more of us than many people realise[20]. The dialogic coach may do little else than encourage dialogue and help teams get better at dialogue, because if the team is great at dialogue, it will be great at working through whatever issue the team faces, including aspects of its own functioning.

A cool idea.

3.   Trust – affective and cognitive

We are probably all familiar with the 'trust' equation[21], or versions of it. The trust equation says:

$$\text{Personal trust} = \frac{\text{Credibility} + \text{Reliability} + \text{Intimacy}}{\text{Self} - \text{orientation}}$$

Credibility is the extent to which people think we are knowledgeable. Reliability is the extent to which people believe I will do what I say I will do. Intimacy is the extent to which I think I can share confidential information with someone. Self-orientation is about my motivation – the extent to which others think I'm focussed on my needs vs other's needs. Our task then becomes to enhance our personal credibility, reliability, and intimacy, and demonstrate our commitment to a common cause.

The literature adds new layers to this handy formula. First, it distinguishes between affective and cognitive trust. This is helpful because each form of trust lends itself to different practices the team coach can adopt in order to enhance that form of trust. It also leads to the idea of swift trust, a form of trust that can be co-created in just one working session[22].

Ana Cristina Costa and colleagues summarise the differences between affective trust and cognitive trust[23]. Affective trust is based on levels of emotional investment, genuine care for others, and a sense that this feeling of care is reciprocated. It is about understanding people's motivations, believing in their honourable intentions, and their commitment to your good wellbeing. Cognitive trust, on the other hand, is about the available knowledge concerning someone's competence, reliability, and dependability.

Which is more important? Some would say the two forms of trust are inextricably bound. Some say cognitive trust precedes affective trust. Some say cognitive trust is most relevant to team performance. Whatever the case, each form of trust may be enhanced by quite different means.

Many coaches go straight to affective trust. To build new levels of affective trust requires people getting to know each other better. It requires that people come to understand each other better so they may better interpret why other people behave the way that they do. If, for example, I know that you really dislike conflict, because you have told me stories of conflict from your home and professional lives, I am much more likely to accept your reluctance to come along and talk to our most difficult client. If I don't understand that aspect of you then I may instead attribute your behaviour to laziness or cowardice. Affective trust takes time to develop because it isn't just informational. I come to understand your motivations through your actions, and the conversations we have around those actions. Like a character in a book, the story we tell ourselves about someone isn't really based on what that person tells us about themselves. Instead that story is informed by our observations of people in action, seeing how they respond to all the different challenges that arise daily. Someone might tell you, for example, that they are committed to ensuring everyone gets things done ('there is no I in team'), but whenever I have a stack of work to do at the end of the day, that person still goes home at five o'clock without offering to help. Building affective trust takes time because I not only need to understand your story, but I also need to relate that story to how I experience you in action.

Cognitive trust is more informational and therefore faster to cultivate. When someone new arrives in my team, I know nothing about that person – their competence, reliability, or dependability. August Capiloa and colleagues share eight conversations a team can have through which they can learn more about each other[24], in terms of:

- Their ability to perform their roles.
- Integrity, and a commitment to being fair and principled.
- The extent to which they have other people's interests in mind, vs. being selfish and self-interested.
- Their capacity to communicate with stakeholders affectively.
- Their dedication to the mission.
- Levels of self-awareness, their strengths and limitations.
- Their overall perspective on the work and their previous experiences.
- How likely it is that they will stay calm in a crisis.

In just one session people can share stories and examples to illustrate their previous achievements in similar roles, examples of remaining fair and principled in the face of challenge, times when they've had other people's backs etc.

This is cognitive trust, and it is as important as affective trust. I may truly trust your motivations, for example, but if I don't believe you are competent to perform your role, then overall levels of trust are likely to diminish. Cognitive trust is more fragile than affective trust though, for reasons already explained. Someone may share great stories about how calm they are in a crisis, and that may align with my first impressions of that person, but the moment they lose their temper in a fraught situation is the moment I lose confidence in that particular aspect of the individual.

I find this distinction between the two forms of trust helpful, and it has greatly influenced my practice. In the past I tended to go straight to affective trust, helping people to get to know each other better. Now I have this lens through which to see what might be most useful to the team, I have a broader repertoire of interventions, particularly when working with teams who may not be together very long.

4. Conflict – task and relationship

Some teams I come across say they don't need any support because everyone gets on very well all the time and they never have any conflict. This is when the hairs on my neck start to prickle. We know that for teams to be innovative and creative, and to avoid the perils of 'groupthink', team members need to disagree. They need to be able to express divergent, sometimes conflicting perspectives. Without conflict there will only ever be limited change, creativity, or innovation and teams are unlikely to succeed in a fast changing, dynamic, competitive marketplace. A team that spends its time in total harmony probably isn't a very effective team.

But many of us don't like conflict. We all have experience of others putting us down or diminishing us, and we all have experience of how interpersonal conflict can make teams dysfunctional and how unpleasant it is to work in those teams. So, harmony feels good. How do we address this paradox? We don't like conflict, but we need it.

Many teams find it helpful to differentiate between task conflict and relationship conflict[25–29]. Task conflict arises when team members disagree about the work to be done. Relationship conflict describes interpersonal incompatibilities among team members due to differences in personality, values, and beliefs. The evidence suggests that task conflict is 'good' and relationship conflict is 'bad' (Figure 5.1).

Without room for task conflict, there is no disagreement about the work to be done. Team members don't feel safe to challenge each other as to the best way forward. You have 'groupthink', with mediocre plans and ideas going unchallenged. More effective teams are comfortable engaging in task conflict and know how to engage in respectful challenge. Task conflict can improve or diminish the performance of a team depending on the ability of team members to communicate effectively.

Relationship conflict generally has a detrimental impact on team performance. Differences between people are personalised. Team members label each other, resentment grows, and relationships become untenable. Relationship conflict at the

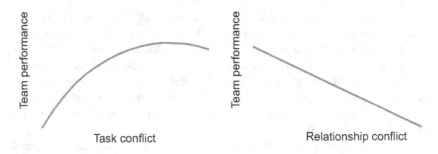

Figure 5.1 Relationships between task/relationship conflict and team performance

early stages of the life of a team can straightaway inhibit information exchange and prevent the team ever reaching even minimal levels of performance[30].

The challenge for the team is that task conflict and relationship conflict tend to co-exist and task conflict may leak into relationship conflict, especially when team performance levels are perceived to be low[31]. People may misinterpret people's intentions and wrongly ascribe malicious intentions to those with who they find themselves in disagreement. Those misattributions lead to relationship conflict. This relationship conflict may be magnified as people start over-identifying with the position they are taking in a debate, such that the position becomes part of their self-identity, and their self-identity becomes something to defend in the face of apparent hostility.

For the team to become more effective, team members must be purposeful as to how they choose to engage in conflict. Many people don't distinguish between task and relationship conflict such that teams may seek to diminish both forms of conflict, to the detriment of performance[32]. Scholars point to the value of team members separating the two constructs in their minds. The literature commends various strategies teams may adopt to better manage conflict through this lens, including education, cognitive reappraisal[33], and various strategies for building trust.

That's the idea. Does it resonate with you?

5.   Diversity – surface level and deep

There is evidence to suggest that companies which manage diversity well perform better. For example, studies have shown that[34]:

- Companies in the top quartile for racial and ethnic diversity are 30% more likely to have above average financial returns.
- Companies in the top quartile for gender diversity are 15% more likely to have above average financial returns.

- Companies in the bottom quartile both for gender and for ethnicity and race are statistically less likely to achieve above-average financial returns.
- In the US, for every 10% increase in racial and ethnic diversity on the senior-executive team, EBIT rose 0.8%.
- In the UK, for every 10% increase in gender diversity on the senior-executive team, EBIT rose 3.5%.

This doesn't mean that enhancing diversity directly leads to performance improvements. Diversity is an *opportunity* to enhance team effectiveness. Diversity brings diversity of perspective, a greater range of options to address any particular challenge, and greater potential for creativity and innovation. But those benefits are only realised if team members collaborate effectively. This is all widely recognised, and many organisations now have programs in place to better manage obvious aspects of diversity, such as age, gender, ethnicity etc.

These programs must be carefully managed if we are to avoid the pitfalls of 'sophisticated stereotyping'. Geoff Abbott and Ingela Camba Kudlow write about paradox[35]. The first paradox is that to choose an intercultural cross-cultural coaching intervention suggests an existing level of awareness already about culture that might make the intervention unnecessary. The second paradox is that to label the intervention as intercultural may undermine its effectiveness because it distracts from other, less obvious, factors. It assumes specific cultural factors can be isolated and treated separately. Abbott and Kudlow talk to the risk that the unskilled well-intentioned coach inadvertently mobilises and reinforces cultural stereotypes in a way that is unhelpful. This is what we mean by sophisticated stereotyping[36]. Sophisticated stereotyping is more informed than low-level stereotyping but can lead to unfortunate outcomes. For example, I was working with a firm in Sydney who wanted people of Asian ethnic origin to have more of a voice. In their new leadership program they decided to divide people into cohorts based on ethnic origin so that people would feel safer to express themselves. Unfortunately, some people felt they were being boxed into categories, sometimes with people with whom they didn't identify, and they resented being defined solely in terms of ethnic origin.

There exist various schema enabling us to characterise people from different countries on several dimensions. Geert Hofstede, for example, defines six cultural dimensions, including power distance, comfort with uncertainty, individualism vs collectivism, etc.[37] It may be helpful to understand that Australians have a relatively low power-distance index compared with Malaysians, which means Australians are less likely to respond well to hierarchy. It may be helpful to know that Slovakians have a high masculinity index and Swedes have a low masculinity index. But not so useful if we assume everyone from a certain country shares these tendencies, or that these are the only aspects of being that we need to pay attention to in order to manage difference.

Age, gender, and ethnicity are all visible aspects of diversity, but we differ from each other in other ways too, aspects of diversity that are less visible. For example, two English people may descend quickly into relationship conflict because one of them went to private school and one of them went to state school, and their experiences in these different learning institutions exposed them to prejudices about each other's systems (e.g. people who go to private schools are over-privileged and entitled, people who go to state schools are uncultured).

The literature differentiates between surface-level diversity, referring to those aspects of ourselves that are relatively easy to observe, and deep-level diversity, which refers to those aspects of self we cannot see, such as values, beliefs, experiences, personality, ways of thinking and looking at the world. Many organisations are focused on surface-level diversity, especially gender and ethnic origin, which is of course important, but there is research to suggest that that deep-level diversity may have the greater potential to impact team performance[38–40]. Your team may have done a lot of work on age, gender, and ethnicity, but that doesn't mean you have a perfect understanding of how diversity plays out in the way you work together. Far from it. There may be all sorts of things going on in the dynamics of such a team based on deep-level diversity.

If diversity on a team is not well-managed, then cracks will appear – or fault lines. Fault lines are like walls, barriers that get in the way of effective communication and collaboration[41,42]. Fault lines inhibit communication, collaboration, alignment, and levels of team engagement and lead to conflict. Obvious fault lines may emerge on the basis of nationality or gender, for example, in which case the team may recognise the need to manage diversity better, but fault lines based on deep-level aspects of diversity may go unrecognised and unaddressed.

I have found this a useful idea, particularly at the moment when there is so much good work going on in the diversity space. These programs do tend to focus on visible aspects of diversity however, such that we may find ourselves distracted from other aspects of difference. As Geoff Abbott suggested, it may be helpful to look at the world sometimes through a lens that says *all* coaching is cross-cultural, because all of our individual identities are at least partly influenced by the cultures of the groups with which we have interacted in the past and interact with now.

What's your perspective?

6. Making it SNOW

Most, if not all, team coaches see part of their role being to work with team dynamics. This means being able to diagnose patterns of behaviour between team members and taking steps to change some of those patterns. This can be a daunting task, depending on what framework the team coach is using. Christine Thornton's perspective on the 'secret life of groups', for example, is both illuminating and complex, based as it is on her expertise in group analysis[43]. A much simpler framework is Bennett Bratt's SNOW model[44]. Bratt's model can be used alongside all and any theoretical models of team dynamics, including Thornton's work. I find this acronym helpful as a generic framework a team can use very easily, to depict their team dynamic in theory-less observable terms.

If we believe that one role of a team coach is to leave the team able to function better without the coach present[45], then we need to find models the team can use by itself, without someone having to become expert in models of team dynamics. The SNOW model is straightforward and provides a space for the team to evolve its capacity to notice and work with increasingly complex aspects of its functioning. SNOW stands for:

See   Make time to notice what's happening
Name   Draw others attention to it
Own   Agree what's happening, align and own behaviours
Work   Experiment with new behaviours

See

We can 'see' through a theoretical lens, or we can simply notice the behaviours themselves, free of theory. If we look through a theoretical lens we may interpret exchanges between people in terms of psychodynamic principles, for example, such as transference and countertransference. Or we might simply notice a behaviour, such as levels of participation in a group, the frequency of interaction between particular individuals, or levels of energy, without having to interpret those behaviours through a theory or framework. As a team gets more comfortable paying attention to what's happening in the room, so levels of observation may evolve. For example, team members may start noticing:

- The extent to which people speak up and listen to each other.
- How people express difference.
- What differences go unexpressed.
- The extent to which conflict appears to be personal or task focused.
- The informal roles that people play.
- Unwritten rules – what is it OK or not OK to say and do?
- The existence of coalitions, sub-groups or cliques and the basis upon which these groupings form.

Name

It is one thing to notice a dynamic, it is another to bring it to the attention of the team. Such conversations can easily degenerate into criticism and debate. It is much harder to talk about team dynamics with other members of the team in a non-judgmental, curious, constructive way. Which may be a place for doing some work on communication and trust.

Own

Once someone has shared their experience of the team dynamic with the group, then it is the task of the group to share experiences, find out what they agree upon and what they don't, and to decide what to do next. In deciding what to do next people must take ownership of their own actions and hold others to account.

Work

Teams often agree to do stuff, and often don't follow through on those actions. This in itself is a function of the team dynamic. If a team is in the habit of agreeing to do stuff and not following through, is this being seen, named, and owned? Team dynamics tend to have a latent pull – a sense of magnetism. If the team doesn't make a determined, collective effort, over a period of time, then the old dynamic may persist.

7.   Structural dynamics

David Kantor's work on structural dynamics provides a relatively simple framework for understanding team dynamics[46]. Kantor's theories of structural dynamics seek to explain the nature of face-to-face communication and illuminate the underlying, largely unconscious structures that underpin verbal exchange. The model is sophisticated enough to allow a team to work at quite a deep level, yet simple enough for a team to learn and work with by themselves. The structural dynamics model is actually three models in one, each of which can be used independently or together. The first model is the Four Player Model.

The Four Player Model

Kantor suggests that *everything* we say can be categorised into one of four buckets:

Move   When we move, we propose a way forward – or invite someone else to propose a way forward.

Follow   When we follow, we support someone else's move, not just nodding silently, but validating the idea and seeing it through to completion.

Oppose   When we oppose, we challenge and correct the 'move'.

Bystand   When we bystand, we provide a perspective on the interaction, either with reference to other things that are going on, or with reference to the way that the team is operating.

Everything we say can be categorised into one of those buckets, based on the underlying intention behind the words. Complimenting someone, for example, may be categorised as a 'follow', an affirmation of what someone has just done. Saying 'thank you' might be categorised as a 'follow', validating the compliment or action, or even a 'bystand', bringing to the conversation an observation of one's gratitude.

So what? What is useful about categorising people's utterances in this way?

Team dynamics form patterns, and those patterns can get stuck. Stuck patterns include:

COURTEOUS COMPLIANCE

One person, often the team leader, makes suggestions and everyone else just agrees. The pattern is move-follow, move-follow, move-follow. No ideas are challenged, and most ideas come from just the one person. Such a pattern is unlikely to lead to innovation or creativity, or to any real degree of quality decision-making.

TO-AND-FRO DEBATE

Debate as a pattern is a repetitive sequence of move-oppose, move-oppose, move-oppose. The focus is on quashing other people's ideas in service of privileging one's own ideas. But few ideas are explored for their potential and value, and there is no alignment around what to do next.

HALL OF MIRRORS

The conversation consists mostly of bystands. Team members are focussed on sharing their observations as to what is happening in the world. The team learns what each other are thinking but attempts to move forwards are often quashed by more observation, often observations as to how challenging the world is and how impossible is the team's task.

SERIAL MOVE

Very common in my experience. Here is there is a lot of energy around moving forward, but everyone has different ideas as to what the team should do next. There is no debate, but nor is there any exploration of other people's ideas. The energy in the room starts high, as people speak with great passion about their own ideas, but tails away as nothing is agreed upon.

COVERT OPPOSITION

People are challenging each other, but doing so in a way that others don't recognise. For example, one team member suggests a particular course of action. Another team member says he finds that idea interesting. He is hoping that, through his tone of voice, others will understand he doesn't think the idea is good enough to pursue, but in fact others assume he means that he thinks the idea is interesting and worth expanding upon. There are many ways of expressing opposition covertly, some deliberate, others less so. The problem with covert opposition is that teams can apparently agree upon a future course of action, when in fact few people are committed to that path.

The Four Player Model provides a simple language through which to identify the pattern (See), bring the pattern to the attention of others (Name), and create possible solutions to change the pattern (Own and Work). For example:

COURTEOUS COMPLIANCE

The pattern is move-follow, move-follow, move-follow. The pattern can be unlocked by someone challenging something proposed (oppose) or bringing the pattern to the attention of the room (bystand) or a combination of both.

TO-AND-FRO DEBATE

The pattern is move-oppose, move-oppose, move-oppose. The pattern can be unlocked by someone inviting others to explore how a particular idea might work (follow) or, again, bringing the pattern to the attention of the room (bystand) or a combination of both.

HALL OF MIRRORS

The pattern is often move-bystand-bystand-bystand-bystand. The pattern can be unlocked by responding to the move (follow or oppose) or, again, bringing the pattern to the attention of the room (bystand).

SERIAL MOVE

The pattern is move-move-move-move. The pattern can be unlocked by responding to the move (follow or oppose) or bringing the pattern to the attention of the room (bystand).

COVERT OPPOSITION

The pattern is unclear. The pattern can be unlocked by enquiring as to what other people are really trying to say.

People can tie themselves in knots trying to work out whether a particular utterance is a move, follow, oppose, or bystand, but beyond establishing a basic understanding as to what each of the four categories mean, such efforts are often wasted. What's important is the pattern, and we don't need to correctly assign every single utterance to spot the pattern. To truly understand the nature of an utterance we need to interrogate what the person is trying to say. Returning to our interesting example, interesting can mean variously:

- I am fascinated by that idea. (Bystand)
- I'm keen on that idea – how do we make it work? (Follow)
- Not in a million years. (Oppose)
- Let's do it. (Move)

The only way to find out the meaning behind the utterance is to ask someone. There will be times in the conversation where it makes sense to stop and ask someone what they are really trying to say, other times when that may not feel necessary, in order to identify the pattern of conversation.

Operating systems

The Four Player Model is useful in itself *and* there are two more models that sit within the broader umbrella of structural dynamics. These next two models enable us to frame people's differences in a way that is both appreciative and constructive.

When we talk about preferred operating systems, we are talking about a preference for:

- Open systems, with an emphasis on collaboration and participation.
- Closed systems, a highly structured way of doing things, with an emphasis on rules, processes, and systems.
- Random systems, with an emphasis on creativity and individuality.

Our task is not to decide which of these systems do I/others ascribe to, because most of us have some propensity for all of these operating systems. It's more about working out which of these propensities may be most prevalent in the situations in which we as a team are working together. Our preferences for different systems show up in the language that we use. For example:

- An emphasis on collaboration and inclusion may indicate a preference for open systems. For example, "before we move on, I'd like to hear what xxx and yyy have to say".
- An emphasis on rules and structure may indicate a preference for closed systems. For example, "can we please make sure we have an agenda for the meeting".
- An emphasis on creativity and new ideas may indicate a preference for random systems. For example, "I've just has a great new idea. I know we don't have much time, but I'd really like to share that idea with you all".

None of these preferences are good and none are bad. All teams require some degree of openness, some degree of structure, and some degree of random creativity. By noticing other people's preferences, it makes it easier to appreciate that preference, even if we feel that preference may be getting in the way of making progress at any given point in time.

Communication domains

We each emphasise different aspects of the world in the way that we communicate:

- Some of us talk most often in terms of relationships and the way people are feeling. This is the domain of affect.
- Others of us talk most often about purpose and ideas – why we are doing things – in service of what? And how else might we think about this situation? This is the domain of meaning.
- And others emphasise results and getting things done. This is the power domain. Notice power doesn't mean wanting to be powerful or being dictatorial. It means a focus on doing things.

Again, a focus on all three domains contributes to the functioning of the overall team. All teams need to connect with each other and with others outside the team (affect). All teams need to step back and think about purpose and consider different ways of thinking about things (meaning). All teams need to get things done (power). But each propensity overplayed can lead to the team becoming ineffective – too much time attending to each other's feelings, too much time spent talking about purpose, too focussed on task. The task of the effective team member is to help the team notice their overall pattern of behaviour, to notice how different members of the team express themselves, to develop a greater respect for people who express themselves differently, and to find an optimal way of working together.

Model clash

Model clash happens when one set of preferred operating systems/communication domains bumps up against another set of operating systems/communication domains. Model clash can generate unhelpful tension in a team. For example:

- George has a preference for closed power. This shows up in his desire to make sure there is a detailed agenda for every meeting. George likes to get things done and gets frustrated if people spend too long talking about ideas or take up too much time expressing their feelings.
- Kelly leans toward open meaning. She likes to ensure everyone has a voice. She thinks the team spends too much time on task, running around like headless chickens. They need to remind themselves what their overall purpose is – why they're there and who they're there trying to serve. From George's perspective Kelly is forever undermining the agenda of meetings, making sure everyone gets to speak!
- Susan has a propensity for random affect. She checks in with others regularly to see how everyone's doing and quickly recognises when people need to take a time-out. She also sees her role as being to throw in new ideas. George experiences Susan as disruptive, always dropping little grenades into the conversation. Kelly wishes Susan was more open to discussing her ideas before throwing them out there.

The tensions between these three people might become the basis for serious relationship conflict, conflict that may de-rail the efforts of the team to perform. By interpreting conflict through the lens of 'model clash' the team may do a better job of enabling people to talk about their differences in appreciative, non-judgmental terms.

I have been referring to Kantor's models and frameworks for many years now. They offer the team a relatively simple means by which to talk about their team dynamics, to create more effective communication patterns, and to manage conflict.

8.   *Taskwork and teamwork mental models*

Most people agree that one role of the team coach lies in helping teams align around a particular purpose, together with strategies, objectives, and goals. Teams also have conversations as to how they will achieve the outcomes they commit to, sometimes in the form of a 'team charter'. The problem in real life is that teams often agree these outcomes and ways of working together, but then go off and act as if those conversations had never taken place.

The literature on taskwork and teamwork mental models provides us with the insights we need to frame the kinds of conversation people need to have if they are to wholly commit themselves to a shared course of action and way of working. A mental model is the lens through which we look at the world. A team mental model is a mental model shared by everyone on a team and is an idea originally articulated by Janis Cannon-Bowers and Eduardo Salas[47]. It includes our understanding of the purpose of the team, the tasks a team is responsible for, how people on a team want to work together, by when tasks need to be achieved, etc. Our mental models are personal, based on our own values, beliefs, and experiences, and they shift and change constantly based on the conversations we have with each other.

There are different kinds of mental model, including:

- Taskwork mental models (what are we here to achieve?).
- Timework mental models (when are we supposed to get things done by?).
- Teamwork mental models (how are expected to work together?).

The distinction between taskwork and teamwork mental models seems especially useful.

Taskwork mental models

Our taskwork mental model addresses the following questions:

- What is our purpose?
- What is our strategy?
- What are our goal and objectives?
- What procedures and policies do we abide by?

It's important that people on a team have the same taskwork mental models. If they don't share the same taskwork mental model, then people will be working to different agendas and seeking to achieve their common tasks by different means. This is likely to lead to disengagement and discord and make it less likely the team will achieve any of its desired outcomes.

Teamwork mental models

Teamwork mental models describe how we work together. Some people, for example, like to work autonomously. They like short, sharp communications with other team members – email is very efficient. They come to work to get the job done, go home, and don't mix home and work. Others are more collaborative. They much prefer to meet face-to-face than use email or telephone. They like to feel close to the people they work with and make time to socialise with work colleagues. If these differences are not surfaced, then whilst these people may agree to be 'collaborative' it's unlikely they will all mean the same thing.

Researchers have shown that teams that have shared mental models are likely to function better and to deliver better outcomes[48]. If teams are to reach a state where leadership is shared, it may be essential for team members to develop shared mental models[49,50].

The process of aligning around particular frameworks may be purely facilitative, making space for conversations around people's existing mental models and co-creating the psychological safety for people to create something that everyone can align with. Robert Hirschfeld and colleagues suggest the process might be educational, assuming it is possible to define best practice and to teach that to everyone on the team[51].

Where does this sit with you? Is this a useful lens to bring to a team, or are you happy to continue going straight to facilitating agreed outcomes without worrying about the role of underlying mental models?

9.   Four dimensions of building a team

As highlighted in Chapter Three, some team coaches don't believe it is their role to work with the team leader individually, or to work with the team at all until the team has been formed. Other team coaches see their role as being broader than that, in which case they may be interested in broadening their understanding of what's required to put together a group of people who are likely to work well together. Those of you who think more broadly may be interested in the work of John Mathieu and colleagues, who proposed four dimensions for building teams[52,53].

Ruth Wageman and Krister Lowe suggest up to 60% of a team's effectiveness is contingent upon the composition of a team[54], yet in many organisations the recruitment process can be quite patchwork, with people struggling to agree even the basic skills and competencies required to fulfil a position. Researchers refer to these basic role attributes as knowledge, skills, attributes, and other characteristics (KSAOs) and traditional job fit models focus exclusively on these KSAOs. Mathieu and colleagues suggest three other lenses through which we can think about building teams[55].

- The traditional model with a focus on the individual's teaming ability added.
- A focus on team profile.
- Recruiting people based on analysis of team dynamics.

Traditional job fit model

The traditional approach to recruitment focuses on the individual's KSAOs. Recruiters often work to a position description, filled in by a hiring manager, detailing those KSAOs. Recruiters often complain how long it takes for hiring managers to clarify what they are looking for, and position descriptions are sometimes vague and unclear. An interview is likely to consist of asking potential recruits to provide evidence of knowledge, skills, and experiences.

Traditional Model + Teaming Ability

This approach is similar to the traditional approach, except it is explicitly recognised that people vary in their motivation and ability to work collaboratively with others. The recruiter is cognisant of the role and the extent to which the potential post-holder needs to be good at teaming. Not everyone has to be great at teaming. Some roles require minimal interaction with other people other than straightforward exchange of information. Other roles demand that the individual can work well with others. In that case potential recruits are asked to provide evidence of their knowledge, skills, experiences, and other attributes – as they apply specifically to teaming.

Team profiling

Our focus now shifts from the individual to the team. This requires looking beyond what's required of the individual in achieving individual goals. What skills do we require at the team level, and what gaps do we need to fill? For example, we have recently had someone leave our team. She had great coaching skills, and role modelled those skills for everyone else on the team. We're about to hire a new person and decide that we need to ensure the new person has great coaching skills and the desire to share those skills with others.

If we ignore the team perspective, then the risk is we end up with a team of great individual performers, all qualified to achieve their technical tasks, all working together well, but underperforming as a team. We may overlook some of the less technical aspects of what is required for this team to be successful, aspects that don't relate to specific roles. In recruiting for new roles, therefore, super-effective teams discuss what skills, experience, and knowledge they may be lacking at a team level, and factor that thinking into recruitment decisions.

Team dynamics

Our focus is again on the team. Through this lens we take into account current team dynamics in hypothesising what characteristics a new person will need to bring to the team if the team is to function well. For example, if certain key clients demand a straightforward communication style, and if the team is composed of two sub-teams who need to work together closely, and if team cohesion is currently strong because everyone likes to socialise every Friday evening after work, then a consideration of these dynamics may be important in selecting a new team member.

It's easy to think of recruitment in overly linear, sequential terms. We build the team, launch the team, then focus on building trust, cohesion, and effectiveness. Once we have built a team and achieved a certain level of trust, we assume that new people will be naturally assimilated and integrated without us having to do very much. This way of thinking leads to problems. When new people join a team, the team dynamic inevitably changes. When existing team members leave a team, the team dynamic inevitably changes. We need to keep our eye on the ball in seeking to build and maintain the right team. We need to anticipate the impact of change, especially if it is unexpected and/or potentially disruptive.

This means paying special attention to new people joining the team and old hands leaving the team. The most effective teams have rituals in place to ensure new entrants are welcomed to the team, and that the team discusses how best to integrate the new person onto current ways of working, including a consideration of the informal roles people play on a team, and the dynamics of the team. Equally the team has rituals to mark the departure of team members, again addressing any gaps that may be left in terms of informal team roles, stakeholder relationships, and team dynamics.

Whether you find this cool idea interesting will likely depend on how you define your role.

10.   Going hybrid – six challenges

When the members of a team are co-located, they often engage in unplanned activities that contribute to the team feeling a sense of togetherness. The team may be quite unaware the extent to which these activities play an important role in team cohesiveness. This doesn't matter so long as nothing happens to significantly change the group dynamic, but the shift from a predominantly face-to-face way of working to a more hybrid model can lead to diminished levels of trust[56] and the team operating less effectively without fully understanding why.

The literature talks of six things that may happen unplanned in a face-to-face team that may not happen as well, or at all, in a virtual or hybrid team.

People get to know each other

In effective teams, people make the time to get to know each other. Often this happens without anyone consciously trying to make it happen. For example, people sit close to each other and witness each other talking to others. They notice what enthuses others and what annoys others. They get a sense of how people like to communicate. They learn about people's personal lives, through noticing the photos on people's desks and screen savers and hearing short stories about what happened this morning, and why people need to leave work early. There are often one or two people on a team who bring people together – without being asked. These are the people who invite everyone down to the pub at the end of the day, or make sure that the Christmas get-together is fun and participative.

In a virtual setting people are less likely to get to know each other without the team making a conscious effort. Someone may need to spot every opportunity to bring the team together face-to-face when possible. Someone may need to explicitly organise meetings that have the sole purpose of getting to know each other – meetings that may feel clunky to some. Someone needs to be encouraging everyone to have their cameras on during meetings and to consider allowing others to view the room in which they are sitting, to feel relaxed when children wander into camera view.

Electronic communication provides fewer social cues and so people make more assumptions about each other's intentions. Conflict may be more likely to arise between team members and the team may need to put in place certain rituals to prevent such conflicts arising and better managing them if they do arise.

In a hybrid team, strategies to build trust include:

- Scheduling in face-to-face time, in a more focused way than just asking people to come to the office x days/week.
- Purposefully connecting and checking-in online at regular intervals.
- Creating specific opportunities for people to get to know each other face-to-face and/or online.
- In the short term, leveraging existing communication channels (cameras on!) and longer term, exploring new digital experiences.
- Noticing and naming inappropriate behaviours early.

People feel part of a (successful) team

Teams are not necessarily 'real' (one of the debates from Chapter Three). We don't pay to join a team or carry around a membership card. If you ask every member of a 'team' who is in that team, you will often get different answers from different people. A team is not a family in which people are related to each other by birth. The team is a construct, something that people talk about, as if it were real, in order to encourage people to feel that they belong to that group. Because when people feel a sense of belonging, they are more committed to other members of that group and perform better.

Teams working face-to-face often sit together in their own 'territory'. People in the team may buy each other coffee and go to lunch together. They may establish certain rituals – such as celebrating each other's birthdays. At social events the team may all choose to dress the same or otherwise signal a formal sense of togetherness. People say things to each other like '*there is no I in team.*'

In a hybrid team, where there isn't always a physical sense of togetherness, members of the team must make special efforts to ensure people feel part of the group. We often hear people who work in purely virtual teams talk about feeling isolated. In an effective hybrid team, team members make a special effort to ensure everyone feels included. This may include initiating virtual versions of some of the rituals that take place in a face-to-face team. It may mean making a special effort to ensure people are aligned round a common purpose and know what each other are doing.

People often have a choice as to which groups they decide to invest their energies in. People like to belong to successful teams. In a virtual world, team members may need to make a special effort to call out success. We tend to notice what needs fixing and overlook what is working well. In successful hybrid teams there is at least the same emphasis on calling out what is working well and dissecting what is working not so well, so that successful behaviours are encouraged and embedded. Strategies to foster a sense of belonging include:

- Making even more effort in aligning people around team goals and ways of working.
- Creating mini projects, appointing people who may not know each other well or don't often work together.
- Being super-attentive to asking everyone for their input.
- Ensuring people know what each other are doing.
- Taking every opportunity to communicate team wins.

People communicate clearly

Establishing good communication practices is super-important in virtual/hybrid teams[57-59]. In effective teams, people communicate with each other often and communicate clearly, but again this often happens without anyone consciously trying to make it happen. When people work together and hear something going on, they can ask questions and offer observations. They engage primarily in verbal communication. When people communicate verbally, people can easily check out whether they have fully understood what others are trying to say. Information is exchanged quickly and easily. People don't have to be great writers – they don't even have to be great speakers, because there is the opportunity for people to quickly test their understanding.

In a virtual setting we may need to be more mindful and purposeful with our communication. People must make a special effort to think about who needs to know what. More communication tends to be written, and so people may need to develop their writing skills. People need to get the balance right between communicating a lot, which can lead to emails being left unopened, and communicating

well. Communicating well may require becoming more skilled and being careful to recognise when it is worth making the effort to engage verbally.
Strategies include:

- Improving people's written skills.
- Establishing clear cadence and structure for communicating.
- Establishing clear communication norms.

People manage conflict

In effective teams, people manage conflict well. This isn't always easy for any team, whether they work face-to-face or virtually, but it is usually harder for virtual teams[60]. This is because teams who work together face-to-face are more likely to build trust, because they are co-located and can get to know each other more easily. Conflict between team members in a face-to-face setting is usually noticed by everyone such that other members of the team are more likely to lean in and play some form of mediator role.

In a virtual team people are more likely to make assumptions about each other's intentions, especially if the team is not good at communicating and if team members are not very good at managing their emotions. Other team members are less likely to witness the conflict in the moment and less likely to step up to mediate. In the virtual setting it may be necessary to train people to better recognise and manage conflict. More time may need to be invested in helping people to get to know each other so that people don't misattribute what other people say and how they behave.
Strategies to consider include:

- Formalising sense-making conversations in response to adversity.
- Helping people understand how to better manage conflict.
- Helping people understand how to better manage their emotions.

People say hello and goodbye

In effective teams, new team members are quickly assimilated into the team. New people are often welcomed and physically introduced to other team members. They get to know other team members without having to try very hard, through being co-located and being able to interact with people informally. They can hear what is going on and ask questions about what they don't understand. If they need help, they can watch for someone to be free then just lean across and ask a question. Some teams do have formal induction processes, but much of the actual induction process is informal and unplanned. When people leave the team there is often some form of ceremony where people can say goodbye and have whatever conversations need to be had.

In a virtual environment it is harder to welcome new people. They don't get to eavesdrop on what's happening. Introductions may be quite formal in a group setting. Without clear process and rituals, it may take people weeks, even months, before they feel like a fully functional team member. Equally, when people depart, whilst there may be an online group event, some conversations may be missed, conversations that are harder to initiate in a group environment. People may leave without speaking individually to some members of the team, because people are so busy.

Strategies include:

- Organising face-to-face meetings for new people to join the team. Make the arrival of new people a special event.
- Building brilliant induction programs. Think hard about who new people need to build relationships with and facilitate the process. Purposefully invite people to shadow others, attend meetings, etc.
- Formally recognise the contribution made by those who leave the team. Make the departure of people a special event too.

People watch out for each other

In effective teams working face-to-face, people are together for most of the day. They have the opportunity to watch out for each other's wellbeing. People may prompt each other to take short breaks; for work conversations, coffee, or just a quick chat. People often go to lunch, or at least eat their sandwiches together. People walk between meetings, saying hello to people and seeing what's going on elsewhere in the office.

Going hybrid changes things. Some people find working from home helps them better manage their wellbeing. They avoid the commute. They may have more time to go for a walk or exercise in the morning. They may find it easier to spend time talking to loved ones etc. On the other hand, some people find working from home more stressful. They may find themselves working non-stop from early morning to late at night. They may live alone or in a small abode with little room to work comfortably. And if the hybrid environment makes working at home more stressful, this may go unnoticed by team members. Life as the member of a hybrid team can be stressful, and that stress may go unnoticed. Being genuinely interested in others wellbeing is particularly important in virtual/hybrid teams[61] .

Hybrid teams can support each other in managing some of that stress by:

- Paying close attention to how individuals are working from home.
- Coaching people to explore new work habits, for example, being more disciplined in switching off from work.
- Ensuring people understand what other support is available and destigmatising (if necessary) the use of support services and asking for help.

- Making time for the team to talk about how they are, and putting the work into building trust.

These are ten cool ideas. Some of these may merit a place in your 'philosophy'.

In the next two chapters I'll look at purpose and practice, the second and third components of the 3Ps.

References

1. Drake, D.B. (2008). Finding Our Way Home: Coaching's Search for Identity in a New Era. *Coaching: An International Journal of Theory, Research and Practice, 1(1)*, 15–26.
2. Santistevan, D. & Josserand, E. (2018). Meta-Teams: Getting Global Work Done in MNEs. *Journal of Management, 45(2)*, 510–539.
3. Mesmer-Magnus, J.R., Asencio, R., Seely, P., & DeChurch, L. (2018). How Organizational Identity Affects Team Functioning: The Identity Instrumentality Hypothesis. *Journal of Management, 44(4)*, 1530–1550.
4. Hirschfeld, R.R., Jordan, M.H., Feild, H.S., Giles, W.F., & Armenakis, A.A. (2006). Becoming Team Players: Team Members' Mastery of Teamwork Knowledge as a Predictor of Team Task Proficiency and Observed Teamwork Effectiveness. *Journal of Applied Psychology, 91(2)*, 467–474.
5. Tannenbaum, S., Mathieu, J.E., Salas, E., & Cohen, D. (2012). On Teams: Unifying Themes and the Way Ahead. *Industrial and Organizational Psychology, 5*, 56–61.
6. De Haan, E., Stoffels, D., Cavicchia, S., Knights, A., Day, A., Bell, J., Sills, C., Tawadros, T., Stubbings, A., Birch, D., & Hanley-Browne, R. (2024). The Future of Team Coaching. In: E. De Haan & D. Stoffels (Eds.), *Relational Team Coaching*. Routledge.
7. Edmondson, A.C. (2011). Teamwork on the Fly. *Harvard Business Review, 90(4)*, 7280.
8. Driskell, J.E., Salas, E., Goodwin, G.F., & O'Shea, P.G. (2006). What Makes a Good team Player? Personality and Team Effectiveness. *Group Dynamics: Theory, Research, and Practice, 10(4)*, 249–271.
9. Amy Edmondson (2012). *Teaming*. Jossey-Bass.
10. Barnett, R.C. & Weidenfeller, N.K. (2016). Shared Leadership and Team Performance. *Advances in Developing Human Resources, 18(3)*, 334–351.
11. Lawrence, P. & Whyte, A. (2017). What do Experienced Team Coaches Do? Current Practice in Australia and New Zealand. *International Journal of Evidence Based Coaching and Mentoring, 15(1)*, 94–113.
12. Clutterbuck, D. (2007). *Coaching the Team at Work*. Nicholas Brealey International.
13. Hawkins, P. (2011). *Leadership Team Coaching: Developing Collective Transformational Leadership*. Kogan Page.
14. Brown, S.W. & Grant, A.M. (2010). From GROW to GROUP: Theoretical Issues and a Practical Model for Group Coaching in Organisations. *Coaching: An International Journal of Theory, Research and Practice, 3(1)*, 30–45.
15. Alrø, H. & Dahl, P.N. (2015). Dialogic Group Coaching – Inspiration From Transformative Mediation. *Journal of Workplace Learning, 27(7)*, 501–513.
16. Bohm, D. (2004). *On Dialogue*. Routledge.
17. Isaacs, W. (2008). *Dialogue: The Art of Thinking Together*. Crown.

18. Lawrence, P., Hill, S., Priestland, A., Forrestal, C., Rommerts, F., Hyslop, I., & Manning, M. (2019). A Dialogic Approach to Coaching Teams. In: D. Clutterbuck, J. Gannon, S. Hayes, I. Iordanou, K. Lowe & D. Mackie (Eds.), *The Practitioner's Handbook of Team Coaching*. Routledge.

19. Lawrence, P., Hill, S., Priestland, A., Forrestal, C., Rommerts, F., Hyslop, I., & Manning, M. (2019). *The Tao of Dialogue*. Routledge.

20. Lawrence, P., Hill, S., Priestland, A., Forrestal, C., Rommerts, F., Hyslop, I., & Manning, M. (2019). *The Tao of Dialogue*. Routledge.

21. Maister, D., Galford, R., & Green, C. (2012). *The Trusted Advisor*. Simon & Schuster.

22. Liu, H.-Y. (2022). The Moderating Role of Team Conflict on Teams of Nursing Students. *International Journal of Environmental Research and Public Health, 19*, 4152–4163.

23. Costa, A.C., Fulmer, C.A., & Anderson, N.R. (2017). Trust in Work Teams: An Integrative Review, Multilevel Model, and Future Directions. *Journal of Organisational Behaviour, 39*, 169–184.

24. Capiloa, A., Baxter, H., Pfahler, M.D., Calhoun, C.S., & Bobko, P. (2020). Swift Trust in Ad-Hoc Teams: A Cognitive Task Analysis of Intelligence Operators in Multi-Domain Command and Control Contexts. *Journal of Cognitive Engineering and Decision Making, 14(3)*, 218–241.

25. Adamovich, M. (2020). The Vicious Cycle of Unfairness and Conflict in Teams. *International Journal of Conflict Management*, 1044–4068.

26. Hartono, B., Dzulfikar, L., & Damayanti, R. (2020). Impact of Team Diversity and Conflict on Project Performance in Indonesian Start-ups. *Journal of Industrial Engineering and Management, 13(1)*, 155–178.

27. Tu, Y. & Zhang, L. (2021). Relationship between Team Conflict and Performance in Green Enterprises: A Cross-Level Model Moderated by Leaders' Political Skills. *Complexity, 2021*, 1–12.

28. Liu, H.-Y. (2022). The Moderating Role of Team Conflict on Teams of Nursing Students. *International Journal of Environmental Research and Public Health, 19*, 4152–4163.

29. Nawaz, M.R., Ishaq, M.I., Ahmad, R., Faisal, M., & Raza, A. (2022). Team Diversity, Conflict, and Trust: Evidence From the Health Sector. *Frontiers in Psychology, 13*, 1–13.

30. Humphrey, S.E., Aime, F., Cushenbery, L., Hill, A.D., & Fairchild, J. (2017). Team Conflict Dynamics: Implications of a Dyadic View of Conflict for Team Performance. *Organizational Behavior and Human Decision Processes, 142*, 58–70.

31. Guenter, H., van Emmerik, H., Schreurs, B., Kuypers, T., van Iterson, A., & Notelaers, G. (2016). When Task Conflict Becomes Personal: The Impact of Perceived Team Performance. *Small Group Research, 47(5)*, 569–604.

32. Humphrey, S.E., Aime, F., Cushenbery, L., Hill, A.D., & Fairchild, J. (2017). Team Conflict Dynamics: Implications of a Dyadic View of Conflict for Team Performance. *Organizational Behavior and Human Decision Processes, 142*, 58–70.

33. Thiel, C.E., Harvey, J., Courtright, S., & Bradley, B. (2019). What Doesn't Kill You Makes You Stronger: How Teams Rebound From Early-Stage Relationship Conflict. *Journal of Management, 45(4)*, 1623–1659.

34. www.mckinsey.com/capabilities/people-and-organizational-performance/our-insights/why-diversity-matters

35. Abbott, G. & Ludlow, I.C. Intercultural Coaching: A Paradoxical Perspective (2024). In: E. Cox, T. Bachkirova & D. Clutterbuck. *The Complete Handbook of Coaching, 4th edition*. SAGE.

36. Osland, J.S., Bird, A., Delano, J., & Jacob, M. (2000). Beyond Sophisticated Stereotyping: Cultural Sense-making in Context. *Academy of Management Executive, 14(1)*, 65–79.

37. Hofstede, G. (2010). *Cultures and Organizations: Software of the Mind, 3rd edition.* McGraw-Hill.

38. Baker, S.D., Saifuddin, S.M., & Stites-Doe, S. (2018). Mending the Gaps: An Exercise in Identifying and Understanding Diverse and Multicultural Team Fault lines. *Organization Management Journal, 15(3)*, 130–143.

39. Bell, S.T. & Outland, N. (2017). Team Dynamics Over Time. *Research on Managing Groups and Teams, 18*, 3–27.

40. Wang et al. (2017). Team Creativity/Innovation in Culturally Diverse Teams: A Meta-Analysis. *Journal of Organizational Behaviour, 40*, 693–708.

41. Baker, S.D., Saifuddin, S.M., & Stites-Doe (2018). Mending the Gaps: An Exercise in Identifying and Understanding Diverse and Multicultural Team Fault lines. *Organization Management Journal, 15(3)*, 130–143.

42. Gibbs, J.L., Sivunen, J.L., & Boyraz, M. (2017). Investigating the Impacts of Team Type and Design on Virtual Team Processes. *Human Resource Management Review, 27*, 590–603.

43. Thornton, C. (2016). *Group and Team Coaching: The Secret Life of Groups, 2nd edition.* Routledge.

44. Bratt, B.H. (2020). *The Team Discovered. Dialogic Team Coaching.* BMI Series.

45. Clutterbuck, D., Gannon, J., Hayes, S., Iordanou, I., Lowe, K., & Mackie, D. (2019). Introduction: Defining and Differentiating Team Coaching from Other Forms of Team Intervention. In: D. Clutterbuck, J. Gannon, S. Hayes, I. Iordanou, K. Lowe & D. Mackie (Eds.), *The Practitioner's Handbook of Team Coaching.* Routledge.

46. Kantor, D. (2012). *Reading the Room.* San Francisco: Jossey-Bass.

47. Mohammed, S. & Dumville, B.C. (2001). Team Mental Models in a Team Knowledge Framework: Expanding Theory and Measurement Across Disciplinary Boundaries. *Journal of Organizational Behavior, 22*, 89–106.

48. Mathieu, J.E., Heffner, T.S., Goodwin, G.F., Salas, E., & Cannon-Bowers, J. (2000). The Influence of Shared Mental Models on Team Process and Performance. *Journal of Applied Psychology, 85(2)*, 273–283.

49. Aufegger, L., Shariq, O., Bicknell, C., Ashrafian, H., & Darzi, A. (2018). Can Shared Leadership Enhance Clinical Team Management? A Systematic Review. *Leadership in Health Services, 32(2)*, 309–335.

50. Bell, S.T. & Outland, N. (2017). Team Composition Over Time. *Research on Managing Groups and Teams, 18*, 3–27.

51. Hirschfeld, R.R., Jordan, M.H., Feild, H.S., Giles, W.F., & Armenakis, A.A. (2006). Becoming Team Players: Team Members' Mastery of Teamwork Knowledge as a Predictor of Team Task Proficiency and Observed Teamwork Effectiveness. *Journal of Applied Psychology, 91(2)*, 467–474.

52. Mathieu, J.E., Tannenbaum, S.I., Donsbach, J.S., & Alliger, G.M. (2014). A Review and Integration of Team Composition Models: Moving Toward a Dynamic and Temporal Framework. *Journal of Management, 40(1)*, 130–160.

53. Tannenbaum, S. & Salas, E. (2021). *Teams That Work: The Seven Drivers of Team Effectiveness.* Oxford.

54. Wageman, R. & Lowe, K. (2019). Designing, Launching, and Coaching Teams: The 60-30-10 Rule and its Implications for Team Coaching. In: D. Clutterbuck, J. Gannon, S. Hayes, I. Iordanou, K. Lowe & D. Mackie (Eds.), *The Practitioner's Handbook of Team Coaching*. Routledge.

55. Mathieu, J.E., Tannenbaum, S.I., Donsbach, J.S., & Alliger, G.M. (2014). A Review and Integration of Team Composition Models: Moving Toward a Dynamic and Temporal Framework. *Journal of Management, 40(1)*, 130–160.

56. Breuer, C., Huffmeier, J., & Hertel, G. (2016). Does Trust Matter More in Virtual Teams? A Meta-Analysis of Trust and Team Effectiveness Considering Virtuality and Documentation as Moderators. *Journal of Applied Psychology, 101(8)*, 1151–1177.

57. Feitosa, J., Grossman, R., & Salazar, M. (2018). Debunking Key Assumptions About Teams: The Role of Culture. *American Psychologist, 73(4)*, 376–389.

58. Feitosa, J. & Salas, E. (2020). Today's Virtual Teams: Adapting Lessons Learned to the Pandemic Context. *Organizational Dynamics, 50(1)*, 1–4.

59. Marlow, S.L., Lacerenza, C.N., & Salas, E. (2017). Communication in Virtual Teams: A Conceptual Framework and Research Agenda. *Human Resource Management Review, 27*, 575–589.

60. Liao, C. (2017). Leadership in Virtual Teams: A Multilevel Perspective. *Human Resource Management Review, 27*, 648–659.

61. Connelly, C.E. & Turel, O. (2016). Effects of Team Emotional Authenticity on Virtual Team Performance. *Frontiers in Psychology, 7*, 1336.

Chapter 6

The 3Ps – purpose

In Chapter Five I invited you to review your philosophy of team coaching. Which of your values and what life experiences shape who you are as a team coach? And what theories, models, and frameworks most resonate for you? In this chapter I'll encourage you to build on those insights in articulating your purpose for doing the work – why do you do team coaching? Team coaching is hard. Alison Hodge and David Clutterbuck write about team coaches feeling that they have been 'badly mauled'[1]. So why do we do it?

Some people look at me a bit puzzled when I ask them why they do team coaching. They say something like – to help teams work better together. Sure – but why? Peter Jackson and Tatiana Bachkirova say we need to dig deeper to truly understand our motivations[2]. They suggest some questions designed to help us further explore our purpose.

I thought it would be helpful if I asked some practising team coaches to share their purpose with us. I sent emails to coaches who had participated in research with me before, to those who had attended our *Team Leader Instruction Manual* accreditation program, and to other coaches I know in the industry. I also posted in LinkedIn. I received responses from 51 team coaches. Half the respondents were male and half were female. They live in Australia, New Zealand, Europe, the US, and India, with the majority being based in Australia and the UK.

I asked them to tell me what their purpose was for coaching teams and invited them to answer some follow-up questions if they had time, questions borrowed and/or adapted from Jackson and Bachkirova's questions:

- What do you hope to achieve with and for the client, the client system, or wider stakeholders? To which of these parties/'systems' are you most committed?
- When contracting with a client how would you know that you could add value to their team?
- What would tell you that your long-term coaching of a team has been successful or at least worthwhile?
- What would tell you that a team coaching session has been a good one?
- On what basis would you say that a team coaching session was a waste of time?
- On what basis would you stop coaching a team?

DOI: 10.4324/9781003546108-7

First, I'd like to thank all those people who responded. I felt very privileged, honoured, and grateful to all, including the vast majority of respondents who took the time to answer the follow-up questions as well. In reading through their responses, please note that all these people have busy lives and they all responded within just a few days.

I've listed every purpose received in the appendix. I edited just a few of the longer ones. There are only 48 items in the appendix because three respondents answered all the follow-up questions but didn't provide an overall purpose.

An explicit purpose

A few respondents didn't articulate an explicit purpose as such (e.g. items 7, 18, and 42). Instead, they provided an account of what they do in coaching and their purpose was more implied. This isn't unusual, according to Jackson and Bachkirova, who say it is common for people to initially mesh what we do with what we hope to achieve through doing it. That may be a useful insight for you, helping to frame your purpose for team coaching. Focussing on what you do may be helpful, but don't forget to then go and consider why you do it.

Focus

A few people wrote about wanting to help the team become more cohesive, without saying why (e.g. items 1, 4, 16, and 17). We might think the reason is obvious, that they want to help the team to perform better, but that isn't necessarily the case. Not everyone who went into more detail was primarily focussed on team performance. Some respondents focussed on the benefits of working with a team for the individual (e.g. items 2, 20, and 25).

> I do team coaching in the hope I can make some small positive impact in the terrible results we see annually in the Gallup 'State of Work' report. Life at work should not be having such a negative impact on people's well-being.
>
> item 20

> My reason for coaching (organisations/teams/individuals) is to have a positive global impact on patients' health (live better, longer/more people) and, at the same time help my clients and me become better versions of ourselves.
>
> item 25

Some people talked about coaching teams as part of individual assignments, in which case it wouldn't necessarily surprise to hear that those coaches are primarily focussed on the outcome for their client.

Others wrote explicitly about wanting to help the organisation (e.g. items 8, 11, 19, 22, 27, and 41).

I do team coaching because supporting the development of high performing teams is very important for organisations and its staff members.

item 8

I choose to work as a team coach because it amplifies the impact I can have within an organisation.

item 11

And some articulated an even broader agenda (e.g. items 5 and 6):

At my core, I am driven by the vision of mending a fragmented society and fostering an environment where 'togethering' (coming together to work side by side) becomes the norm rather than the exception. My ultimate goal is to overcome the pervasive 'story of separation' that plagues modern society.

item 6

What is your primary motivation in coaching teams? In considering the question you may immediately go to a focus on helping the team. Again, that may be what you are doing, but is that why you are doing it?

Philosophy

In exploring our 3Ps Peter Jackson and Tatiana Bachkirova suggest that the most logical place to start may be philosophy because it is our philosophy, our system of beliefs and assumptions, that informs both our purpose and practice. In support of that notion we can see aspects of respondent's values, experience, and theory show up in their purpose. Item 5 speaks to a strongly held value, for example:

Fundamentally I believe we can achieve more together than we do alone.

item 5

Item 2 is a good example of someone's values *and* previous experience showing up in their purpose:

I know what bad looks like, and even in a position of influence felt powerless. I had to go. I want nobody to have to go through that. That drives me. Equity, fairness, being a good human.

item 2

Items 6, 19, 24, 36, 39, and 46 refer specifically to a belief. For example:

My deeper purpose stems from a belief in the inherent goodness of people and the transformative power of collaboration.

item 6

I do team coaching because of my belief in the wisdom that teams hold, and often, that is underrated. My purpose is to unleash the team's wisdom so that it realises its potential by taking progressive action.

item 36

My purpose is grounded in the belief that aligned teams who share a common purpose, can change the world for the better.

item 39

In terms of theories and frameworks, item 43 makes multiple references to systems theories, in particular David Kantor's work on structural dynamics. Item 29 talks to theories of team dynamics and systems. Item 10 makes specific reference to the work of Foucault and Deleuze and Guattari. Item 22 refers to vertical development theories, specifically the work of Lev Vygotsky.

Having thought already about your philosophy, how do those insights help you to inform your purpose?

Delving deeper

The follow-up questions helped surface other aspects of purpose.

1.   What do you hope to achieve with and for the client, the client system, or wider stakeholders? To which of these parties/systems are you most committed?

The answers to this question again shed more light on the respondent's purpose with regard to scope. Most respondents switched focus at this point to the needs of stakeholders. For example:

Each partnership is unique, and we'll contract for the outcomes that are important for them. As part of building the brief we take questions to explore what success might mean and what assumptions they're making about what the issue/challenge/root cause is.

Who though are the stakeholders? Some respondents focused primarily on the team. For example:

I am primarily committed to the team. The relationships with other stakeholders are key elements of context and need careful and early negotiation.

I am most committed to the team, as it is the space and entity in which individual and organisational performance and wellbeing can be most affected.

At the moment my work is focused on the team I work with, helping them to uncover what matters which exists in their wider system.

Some focussed explicitly on the business or 'eco-system':

> I hope to achieve a long-term sustainable way to work together, to achieve the goals of the business. I have found by taking the business as the focal point, it creates a space for people to depersonalise the conflict and focus on a neutral and common purpose. I find that all stakeholders tend to benefit, as a result.

> I would like to think I keep the whole eco-system in mind, and I appreciate that the vehicle for change is often the people with whom I am working in the room to influence their system.

How does this question help you further understand your purpose?

2. When contracting with a client how would you know that you could add value to their team?

The answers to this question provided insights on philosophy, in particular some of the underlying beliefs that underpin the team coach's work, both generally and in terms of what areas the team might want to focus on. Not surprisingly, several coaches talked about the commitment and capacity of the team to do the work. For example:

> My clients have enough self-awareness, humility and commitment to want to change.

> If they are a team willing to be reflective and work within themselves.

> To what extent the briefing meeting goes beyond the superficial, i.e. the sponsor isn't saying 'we'd like you to do this because of y' with no room to explore.

But it wasn't just about the team being willing and able. Some coaches talked about other factors they said must be present if an assignment is to succeed:

> I will not take on the work if the combination of toxicity, resourcing commitment, and leadership issues are too limiting.

> When I hear that they are approaching difficult conversations that in the past they by-passed.

Some talked about their personal capacity and organisational fit.

> Part sense of 'fit' with the culture. I also hold a sense of the size and scale of the complexity to which I can work in. Sometimes I sense assumptions about my age, experience, seniority, will mean some team members will engage better or worse with a different team coach.

Some spoke about wanting to understand the team leader's philosophy on team and on leadership, and on areas of team effectiveness that would have most impact. If the team coach was to be successful, he/she wanted to be aligned philosophically with the team leader.

> I'm always curious to understand the client's definition of team coaching and why they think it will add value to the organisation.

> The team leader wants to learn more about leading their team to be more autonomous.

> If the client is talking about design, launch and operating a team in areas of team purpose, team dynamics, team objectives, alignment of team members.

Others took a more emergent perspective, saying that the value of the work could only become apparent over time. For example:

> I don't think that I would presume to 'know' that I could add value, which I believe should be emergent and derived from the actions of the team and I would share this vulnerability with the sponsor and the team.

How does your philosophy steer the choices you make in determining whether you think you can bring value to a team? And if not clear, do you walk away from the assignment, or take the work anyway and see what emerges?

3.   What would tell you that your long-term coaching of a team has been successful or at least worthwhile?

This is a great question in helping you better understand why you do the work. What constitutes a successful outcome for you? And what if the outcome you look for is different to how the client is defining success?

Jackson and Bachkirova talk about the challenges for the coach in not projecting their individual purpose onto the client regardless of the client's stated need, and conversely, not focussing exclusively on the client's need regardless of what the team coach thinks needs to happen. In other words, balancing what each party thinks will be the best outcome for the team.

A few respondents defined success only in terms of client satisfaction. For example:

> Subjective reports from participants, team performance and relationships.

At the other end of the spectrum some respondents talked only about measures reflecting a personal belief as to what an effective team looks like, without discussion of specific teams and their context:

> I know if the team is being successful if they are not only working on their task but are also discussing their vulnerabilities, results of 360 feedback with each other and able to provide feedback to one another in a psychological safe way.

The team have raised their awareness of their patterns of practice and have the insight to shift towards new ways of engaging with each other.

I start hearing them taking more systemic perspectives.

Many talked about the contracting process and agreeing metrics with the client at the beginning of the assignment, bringing together client and coach definitions of success:

Measurement against agreed outcomes with team and sponsor. Feedback gathered through scaling, survey, discovery convos, end of coaching reflections.

The team is either achieving, or on track to achieve, its coaching objectives. Agreed measures and milestone would either be met, on track, or re-calibrated, based on what was discovered.

Specific success indicators are well defined prior to the team coaching engagement Success would be a combination of positive changes in the team assessments and meeting the goals/outcomes agreed with the team/organisation.

These perspectives don't elaborate as to how the team coach effectively contracts. The coach may find it hard to disentangle their needs from the needs of the client:

How do you differentiate your bias from your client's needs? Who is your client? How do you disaggregate from your own thinking? Navigating the complexity of the person in front of you and the organisation is an oft hidden complexity that confounds even the best of us. Still learning how to navigate this one … help!

One respondent said he didn't set team coaching goals in isolation, that the assignment had to be established with reference to the organisational agenda:

My approach to the work now is that I am very unlikely to take on team coaching in isolation. I prefer only to do work it is a part of striving for an important strategic goal. The measurement then comes as part of assessing the progress of that strategic objective.

How then do you define success? And how do you navigate your sense of what needs to happen with the client's sense? Or do you just focus on giving the client what they ask for? If you do contract, to what extent are you aware of your own beliefs and biases and how do you manage those?

4.   What would tell you that a team coaching session has been a good one?

On the face of it a very similar question. But in this instance the judgment is more spontaneous, unlikely to be informed by metrics agreed for the overall assignment. Again, do you tend to go external or internal, or both?

Some respondents referred primarily to the team's experience. If they were happy, then the coach was happy.

> How engaged each team member was, what they said about the session in team reflections, how the sponsor described their reflections a few days later.

Others went internal, again revealing personal beliefs as to what constitutes successful team coaching:

> Talking/getting into issues that previously have been avoided. Improved above-the-line behaviours by leader/team members/team as a whole.

> When the team has recognised unconscious patterns and has the energy to shift towards new patterns.

> There has to be a lot of disturbance, awkward moments, lots of emotion, regret, excitement, amazing discovery, vulnerability episodes.

Some were wary of rating individual sessions at all. For example:

> I find this hard to answer as the value of the work happens over time rather than in a single session.

> I think you might get a very different answer depending on when you ask the question, as it may take a while for the full impact to sink in. So, a session which may not have seemed very useful at the time may subsequently turn out to be hugely useful.

How do you decide if a session has gone well? Is it enough that the team say they found it useful? Or do you need to see something happening? And how do you manage your audience if they say they didn't find it helpful, but you think the session may have been good for them, or if you think it may be potentially helpful depending on their later response?

5. On what basis would you say that a team coaching session was a waste of time?

Some people talked about an apparent lack of energy in the room, implying a direct connection between overt enthusiasm and the achievement of desired outcomes.

> When I don't feel the rapport or interest is there.

> If it feels like we were going through some motions, not fully committed to the work. Aiming for a 'nice day' feels like a waste of time to me.

Some refuted the idea that any single session ought to be regarded as a waste of time, emanating perhaps from perspectives on team dynamics and systems. For example:

Even if there is reluctance in the room to move forward, that is a discussion. If there is anger or disagreement, that is a discussion. If there is no alignment, that is a discussion. If there are poor relationships that need work, that is a discussion. So, I would never consider it a waste of time.

It is very hard to say a session was a waste of time as there are many interactions that will not show an impact until a future time. Even if the team said it was a waste of time that would open a discussion that would most likely lead to a positive shift or change.

What is your immediate thought in reflecting upon this question? Thinking more deeply on the question, with reference to your philosophy of team coaching, do your thoughts take you somewhere different?

6. On what basis would you stop coaching a team?

Whilst some respondents may be curious as to the lack of engagement in a single session, most said that a more general commitment to the purpose of the work is required. For example:

I wouldn't necessarily stop but I would recontract and possibly shift to other approaches if there is team wide rejection of the approach, not going anywhere, not clear on what they're looking to achieve.

If the team were not engaged in the work – I'd explore what was causing this before stopping.

Some respondents talked about stopping because they weren't achieving the outcomes *they* sought:

They stop experimenting (or never start). If even after I point out the pattern, they just keep talking about stuff instead of entering into the experience of doing it. They are not interested in learning new ways. They are comfortable in their old ways.

A team is a living system. There must be some acknowledgement that their own system and context is getting in the way of progress.

Some talked about stopping the work because the work was done:

My aim is to get the team coaching themselves. It is developmental, but I would recommend for them to continue after the formal engagement is finished.

But who decides if the work is done? Sometimes the coach:

Once they are at the level of articulating their own shared team values, code of conduct, manifesto – call it what you will – their words and their commitment to one another- then exit right!

Other times it may not be so clear:

The law of diminishing returns should occur in any time frame of team coaching so this should at least pause coaching until new circumstances suggested further returns. But then what are the 'returns' and who decides on them?

Your purpose

It's easy to talk about what you *do* as a team coach when asked about purpose, or to talk in very general terms – *because I want to help teams work better together*, for example. But these answers don't explain why you do the work. It's helpful to understand why you do team coaching, and useful for potential clients. Do your aspirations match their aspirations? So, I suggest spending some time digging a little deeper. Why is it important to you to help teams work better together? Is it really teams that you want to help, or is your purpose ultimately to help organisations to be more successful? Or are your aims more societal? How do your life experience and your values show up in your purpose? To what extent is your purpose determined by ideas and theories, such as systems theories or theories as to the nature of the way people work together? And once you have achieved further clarity of purpose, how does this help you determine which clients to work with? To what extent does your purpose have to align with their purpose?

My purpose

Before we move on, let me share with you where I think my own purpose has got to. When I set out as a team coach, I think my purpose was to help teams work together more cohesively in service of becoming more effective. I think I held a somewhat simplistic perspective on how organisations work, along the lines of – the more teams there are that work effectively, the more likely it is that the organisation as a whole will work effectively. And so my focus was on the team I was working with and its internal dynamics, informed by ideas on group functioning I learned in completing my training in counselling and therapy, including group therapy.

Over the years, through experience and exploring various systems theories, I became less convinced that I was always adding value in focussing only on the team and its stakeholders. I developed a perspective, informed both by experience and theory, through which I saw the organisation as a great network of people, all moving in and out of each other's worlds. To help this great *shoal* of people to become more collectively purposeful and impactful would require me and others to take a whole-shoal approach. I worked with teams who became really very skilled at working with each other and with their external stakeholders, but still things didn't shift. Patterns emerged in my mind, of my touching fragments of this vast ever shifting shoal of people. That didn't mean I didn't think my work was worthwhile, only that I might usefully rethink on occasion the nature of a best intervention. My purpose shifted more toward developing a better understanding of the whole, in order to help the team, in order to help the whole.

My purpose shifted again in conducting the meta-research referred to in the Introduction and in Chapters Three and Five of this book. As I worked through these readings and sought to integrate them with my hands-on experience in service of creating something I hoped would be useful for others, I was struck one day by a thought. Why develop this material solely for external coaches? Why not develop the material so that any leader can pick up these tools and use them with his/her team? Indeed, why aim only at the team leader? Inspired by the ideas around meta-teaming – why not skill up an entire organisation to be good at teaming?

There exists contemporary research to suggest that helping leaders to become better team coaches may be more impactful than providing external team coaching[3]. I realised that my commitment these days is to the bigger entity and that to distinguish always between individual, team, and organisation coaching, and to suggest that one or other is more useful, doesn't feel helpful. If the shoal is forever shifting and evolving, then every touchpoint is potentially insightful. It may be most appropriate to think of individual, team, and organisational interventions as all being potentially helpful. The art (or the science if you prefer) lies in choosing when to do what, in consultation with your client. I realised there is no way of objectively determining whether an intervention is successful. The success or otherwise of an assignment is a story told by people across an organisation, and people will coalesce and form coalitions around different perspectives and those different perspectives are constantly emerging, interacting, and evolving. I can usefully pay attention to the evolution of these stories and engage directly with the storytellers to work out how best to tweak the intervention.

So, my purpose for team coaching then has become something along the lines of working with a team, whilst simultaneously working with other parts of the shoal, to enhance relationship, understanding, and collective effectiveness.

Today, anyway.

Now you have had a think about your philosophy and purpose, we'll move to practice. After all, we ultimately need to translate all this into something practical and tangible. As Jackson and Bachkirova say:

> If, for example, you have a personal commitment to serving the profession or humanity as a whole, this ultimate purpose has to be translated into something more concrete which allows you and [your client] to have reasonably clear expectations of what the progress or lack of it would look like.
>
> Jackson and Bachkirova (2019)

References

1. Hodge, A. & Clutterbuck, D. (2019). Supervising Team Coaches: Working with Complexity at a Distance. In: D. Clutterbuck, J. Gannon, S. Hayes, I. Iordanou, K. Lowe & D. Mackie (Eds.), *The Practitioner's Handbook of Team Coaching*. Routledge.
2. Jackson, P. & Bachkirova, T. (2019). The 3Ps of Supervision and Coaching: Philosophy, Purpose and Process. In: E. Turner & S. Palmer (Eds.), *The Heart of Coaching Supervision. Working with Reflection and Self-Care*. Routledge.
3. Traylor, A.M., Stahr, E., & Salas, E. (2020). Team Coaching: Three Questions and a Look Ahead: A Systematic Literature Review. *International Coaching Psychology Review, 15(2)*, 54–68.

Chapter 7

The 3Ps – practice

In Chapter Five I threw around some ideas in service of helping you think further about your philosophy. In Chapter Six I shared with you what 51 practising team coaches said to me was their purpose. In this chapter I'll round off the 3Ps by considering how philosophy and purpose show up in practice.

The practice piece is about what you actually do. If someone were to shadow you for a few months, what would they see you doing upon your initial engagement with a stakeholder, through to conducting some kind of diagnosis (if you do diagnoses) through to starting work with the team and progressing through the assignment? What would that person see you do, and how would those behaviours connect back to your philosophy and practice?

Areas to think about

We might start with some of the questions raised in Chapter Three, questions relating especially to contracting. Questions such as:

- How big a team am I prepared to work with?
- How will I decide on a pattern of working with a team?
- Do I work with teams where a lot of the team members belong to other teams too, and may only be able to attend some sessions and not others?
- Will I build individual coaching into my overall recommendation?
- Will I work alone or with others?

These are just some questions you will want to consider. You will have other areas to think about in terms of how you go about doing the work. For example:

- How do you approach the initial briefing meeting? What kinds of questions will you ask? How will you describe what you do? What boundaries and parameters will you set?
- Which stakeholders do you want to talk to and when? What kind of relationship do you want with the team leader? Do you want to talk to any of the team's stakeholders before agreeing to do the work?

DOI: 10.4324/9781003546108-8

- What else do you want to cover in your initial contracting?
- How will you and your stakeholders define success and how will you measure progress?
- Will you conduct some form of diagnosis before meeting the team?

And so on. Now would be a good time to go to a few workshops and seminars, listen to some podcasts and read a few books. Lucy Widdowson and Paul Barbour's book is full of tools and techniques[1], as is Georgina Woudstra's book[2], and the book by Erik de Haan and Dorothee Stoffels[3], and many more besides. Find out what others do and evaluate those practices through the lens of your philosophy and purpose. Not all writers or practitioners articulate the rationale behind what they do, which can make it hard to understand why they do what they do, but listening to what they do through your lens provides you all the context you need to work out the extent to which their practical recommendations are likely to sit well within your own personal approach to team coaching.

Translating philosophy and purpose to practice – an example

In the rest of this chapter, I'll share a personal example of how aspects of my practice evolved from insights gained in reconsidering my philosophy and purpose. As I've shared already, a few years ago I conducted a major overhaul of my approach to team coaching. I read academic articles, read books, and talked to other team coaches. From that work emerged the perspective on debates detailed in Chapter Three. I did all of that work only in service of enhancing my practice. I wasn't interested in writing a purely conceptual, academic text on team coaching. I wanted to extract practical insights from that work.

As well as extracting the material on debates and cool ideas, I conducted a thematic analysis of all the articles and books I read. The team effectiveness literature cites a lot of models, but I was more interested in digging into the models to understand underlying theories and working out how to translate those theories into simple, practical tools and methodologies.

In reading through the literature and some of the associated literature on systems I had studied previously[4,5,6], I came up with 13 broad themes. These then became the category headings under which to organise a vast collection of ideas and frameworks for working with teams. The 13 themes were:

Leadership style. The literature reviews different ways of leading and the impact of the leader's adopted style and the performance of the team. The literature often advocates for the effectiveness of shared leadership models when attempting to address complex issues and working virtually or hybrid.

Communication. Studies around the importance of communication between team members. Includes material on listening, respectful voicing, and the emotional management required to be able to engage with someone most effectively.

Team development. Most notably the Tuckman model and challenges to that mode, and the work of Connie Gersick (Chapter Three)[7,8].

Building Trust. How to enhance levels of trust through focussing on individual behaviours, team behaviours, and the organisational context. The value of distinguishing between cognitive trust and affective trust.

Swift Trust. Most relevant to teams that come together to achieve short-term goals. How to build levels of cognitive trust quickly.

Managing Conflict. Studies pointing to the importance of teams being able to manage conflict well if they are to perform to their potential. The value of distinguishing between relationship conflict and task conflict.

Team Alignment. Alignment around purpose, goals and objectives, and ways of working together. The notion that alignment requires us to build shared mental models within the team, around taskwork (what we are here to do) and teamwork (how we will work together to achieve those goals).

Team Dynamics. Yes – with reference to Chapter Three I did decide that team dynamics are an important part of team coaching for me, based on my own experiences in the field. David Kantor's work on structural dynamics was most pertinent here[9].

Managing Diversity. The value of distinguishing between surface-level diversity and deep-level diversity. Helping people to recognise and manage the assumptions they make.

Systems and Politics. Drawing on previous meta-research into systems theories and how different systems theories underpin different ways of thinking about change[10].

Going Hybrid. How to help a hybrid team function to its full potential.

Multi-Team Membership. How to best manage a team when members of the team are also members of other teams. Particularly relevant to professional services firms.

Building a Team. Yes – with reference to Chapter Three, I chose to adopt a broad scope when working with teams. This theme includes work by John Mathieu and colleagues looking at more 'systemic' ways of thinking about team recruitment[11].

It occurred to me in identifying this list of themes, that many coaches tend to focus on just a few of these themes because they are the ones they learned in training. If my training emphasised the importance of aligning on common purpose and goals, for example, then I may direct the team to focus on alignment, even if their core area of struggle might be something entirely different, such as how to work together effectively as a hybrid team. Or if my training focussed mostly on team dynamics, that might be where I go, regardless of the team's needs. Identifying these themes has enabled me to invite the team to choose their own path toward becoming more effective. I feel much more adaptable and responsive to the needs of the clients I work with.

As I explained in Chapter Six, as I worked through the rebuilding of my approach to team coaching, I felt the purpose of the work change for me. I realised that my purpose going into the exercise was something around helping teams to become more effective. As I reflected on some of the narratives around teams and meta-teams, and the value in being able to work effectively in a world of fluidity and change, my purpose shifted to something more scaled; being able to enhance the capacity of leaders at all levels to work with their teams. We have been helping leaders to coach their own people one-to-one for years, I realised. Now is the time to start helping those same leaders to coach their teams, to coach on a one-to-many basis, a theme echoed by several contributors to Erik de Haan and Dorothee Stoffels' book on relational team coaching[12]. My purpose shifted from being a good team practitioner, to being a good practitioner *and* helping organisations build that capacity in-house. In most of the organisations I have worked in, it's only the leadership team who tend to benefit from team coaching. How might we help *every* team in an organisation to become more effective?

This purpose pushed me to come up with tools and methodologies that could be applied by team leaders who have never received any training whatsoever in team coaching. They would need to have good people skills and the capacity to structure and deliver a team session, but they wouldn't need to have an expertise in team dynamics, or a background in conflict management or stakeholder management. From this insight emerged the Team Leader Instruction Manual (TLIM).

Team Leader Instruction Manual (TLIM)

The Team Leader Instruction Manual (TLIM) is my practice model written down and made available to other people to use. I structured the 13 themes as shown in Figure 7.1. This diagram may need to be amended at some point – I certainly hope so. People will point out holes and gaps and suggest new themes. All of which is wonderful, because I hope that my personal approach to team coaching will continue to evolve and develop until the day I stop doing the work. The TLIM consists of a manual and more than 30 supporting resources. It's written so it can be used equally by experienced team coaches looking to further build upon their existing expertise, and by team leaders, with no training or experience coaching teams at all. The TLIM is self-published so allowing me, and a growing community-of-practice, to continue to develop it, refining it every 12 months or so.

Each of the 13 themes is a small collection of cool ideas accompanied by specific actions, exercises, and methodologies. Some of those methodologies sit within the literature, others I have made up, others I have been gifted by other coaches, particularly those who have opted to work more with the model.

My first idea was simply to have 13 themes and invite teams to pick where they wanted to go. That became unwieldy for what I now had in mind, because I wanted to put it all on paper in a way that made it easy for others to use, and if every chapter was independent then there would be lots of repetition. And so there emerged a structure that enabled me to avoid repetition. In writing about team

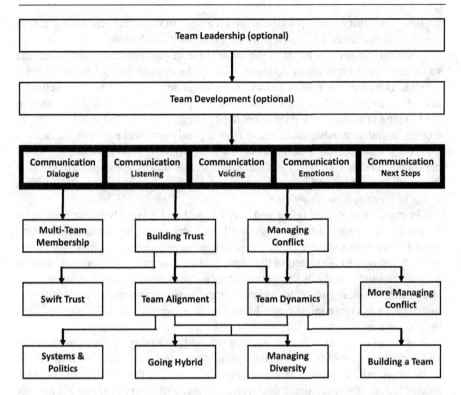

Figure 7.1 The thirteen themes of the Team Leader Instruction Manual (TLIM)

dynamics, for example, and team alignment, and managing diversity, I didn't want to repeat the same materials around the importance of building trust to enable good conversation. And so, building trust comes first and there are lines then leading to the other themes.

You can see aspects of my philosophy featuring in the diagram. You can see a belief in the value of shared leadership evident in the model, for example. Though it may not be explicit, I believe that this kind of work will be easier to work through if the team leader at least adopts a consultative approach to the team. And so, the 'team leadership' component, embracing 'leadership style', sits as part of the overall process in reminding me to have early conversations with the team leader as to how we will all work together most effectively.

The team development aspect comes next, as a potentially useful conversation to have with the team as to where it feels it is on its journey, with reference to Tuckman or Gersick perhaps, or through a different lens if that makes sense to the team. Thinking about where they are on their journey may help them think through what work they want to do together, as well as how often they want to meet, and for how long. But it's an optional theme given that many of the teams I work with are so fluid that team development models don't add much value.

Next you can see my belief in the importance of good communication and the value in sharing ideas about dialogue. Clearly the conversations I had with team coaches as part of my research stuck in my mind somewhere. This sits well with my own personal philosophies around change generally, which is that efforts to lead change in a complex environment depend to an extent on the agent's ability to engage in dialogue. Also, and coming from a purely practical perspective, most of the work a team does in seeking to become more effective requires that team members communicate well with each other. It therefore makes sense to me to position this work to the fore and invite the team to talk about how it talks to itself before trying to talk about anything else.

The model looks quite linear and may be used in a relatively linear fashion by a team leader or novice team coach, but I see more experienced coaches drawing from the materials to create their own quite flexible approaches to building an intervention that best fits the need of the team. A team may not want to spend as much time as the model suggests on communication, for example. They may want to get straight into building trust. In which case the more experienced coach will take materials from communication and build those materials into the design of their session on trust.

This structure, a list of themes each supported by a library of practical exercises and actions, is a means by which to think about and contract around the focus of the work with a team. It is not an attempt to build a definitive team coaching model. It is an approach that I find works for me, and others who share a broadly similar philosophy. It does not say that 'building a team' is definitely in-scope for a team coach. It *does* say that I feel personally comfortable in sharing these ideas around team building with a team and helping them to make sense of them, and take actions based on that understanding.

The TLIM doesn't capture every aspect of practice for me. It doesn't, for example, contain a section on contracting. It represents a 'playbook' if you will, a series of exercises and conversations a team might usefully have in their quest to become more effective. You can see my philosophy showing up again here. My version of a team coach is not limited to sharing in-the-moment observations and questions, as suggested by Alexander Caillet and Amy Yeager[13]. It also includes some exercises, tools, and games – as they might define team facilitation, training, or team building. I don't suggest my perspective is better than theirs, only that it is mine, a perspective that resonates most for me, given my experiences in life.

Back to you

The TLIM is an example of one person translating philosophy and purpose into practice. It may or may not resonate for you. It is more likely to resonate if you think we share similar philosophies and purpose. If your philosophies and purpose are different to mine, then you will want to construct something quite different.

As you continue to do the work and read about the work and listen to podcasts, whose work are you drawn to? What approaches, methodologies, and frameworks appeal? Do you see the value in compiling not only a library of different possible methodologies, but in charting the connections between your values, experiences, favourite theories, and reason for doing the work, into how you do the work? And do you see the value in being able to articulate all of this to people who have expressed an interest in working with you, in service of best agreeing how you will go about doing the work together?

References

1. Widdowson, L. & Barbour, P.J. (2021). *Building Top Performing Teams. A Practical Guide to Team Coaching to Improve Collaboration and Drive Organizational Success.* Kogan Page.
2. Woudstra, G. (2021). *Mastering the Art of Team Coaching.* Team Coaching Studio Press.
3. De Haan, E. & Stoffels, D. (Eds.) (2024). *Relational Team Coaching.* Routledge.
4. Lawrence, P. (2021). *Coaching Systemically. Five Ways of Thinking About Systems.* Routledge.
5. Lawrence, P. (2019). What is Systemic Coaching? *Philosophy of Coaching: An International Journal, 4(2)*, 35–52.
6. Lawrence, P. (2021). Team Coaching: Systemic Perspectives and their Limitations. *Philosophy of Coaching: An International Journal, 6(1)*, 52–82.
7. Gersick, C.J.G. (1988). Time and Transition in Work Teams: Toward a New Model of Group Development. *Academy of Management Journal, 31(1)*, 9–41.
8. Gersick, C.J.G. (1989). Marking time: Predictable Transitions in Task Groups. *Academy of Management Journal, 32(2)*, 274–309.
9. Kantor, D. (2012). *Reading the Room.* San Francisco: Jossey-Bass.
10. Lawrence, P. (2021). *Coaching Systemically. Five Ways of Thinking About Systems.* Routledge.
11. Mathieu, J.E., Hollenbeck, J.R., van Knippenberg, D., & Ilgen, D.R. (2017). A Century of Work Teams in the Journal of Applied Psychology. *Journal of Applied Psychology, 102(3)*, 452–467.
12. De Haan, E., Stoffels, D., Cavicchia, S., Knights, A., Day, A., Bell, J., Sills, C., Tawadros, T., Stubbings, A., Birch, D., & Hanley-Browne, R. (2024). The Future of Team Coaching. In: E. De Haan & D. Stoffels (Eds.), *Relational Team Coaching.* Routledge.
13. Caillet, A. & Yeager, A. (2018). *Introduction to Corentus Team Coaching.* Corentus.

Chapter 8

Team coaching supervision

Where we've been

In Chapter One I questioned the value of an exclusive focus on team coaching competencies and cited Ralph Stacey in advocating the importance of paying attention to practical judgment. We cannot hope to address the challenges of a leader or team coach solely in terms of rules and process. We must acknowledge how unpredictable is the world around us, how our un-formulaic practical judgment is embedded in personal experience. Practical judgment cannot be taught as such, nor can it be reduced to a set of rules. Practical judgment is the experience-based ability to notice what's going on and to intuit what's most important about that situation, and it develops and evolves through experience and reflecting on that experience.

In Chapter Two I advocated for the 3Ps as a simple framework around which to organise our experience and reflections in service of bringing clarity to the way we approach our work, in this case as team coaches. The 3Ps invite us to consider questions around our personal philosophy, purpose, and practice, questions such as:

Philosophy

- What experiences have been most pivotal in you becoming the team coach you are today?
- Which of your values show up in the way you operate?
- What theories, frameworks, and models most inform your practice?

Purpose

- Why do you do team coaching – what is your purpose?
- What do you hope to achieve with and for the client, the client system, or wider stakeholders? To which of these parties/systems are you most committed?
- When contracting with a client how would you know that you could add value to their team?
- What would tell you that your long-term coaching of a team has been successful or at least worthwhile?

DOI: 10.4324/9781003546108-9

- What would tell you that a team coaching session has been a good one?
- On what basis would you say that a team coaching session was a waste of time?
- On what basis would you stop coaching a team?

Practice

- What do you do upon first being asked if you'd be prepared to coach a team?
- In taking the initial brief?
- In seeking to understand the needs of different stakeholders?
- In preparing to meet members of the team for the first time?
- In session with a team?
- In responding should a team apparently disengage with you, or with each other?

This is far from an exhaustive list of questions. The purpose of the exercise is to gain clarity for yourself as to what perspectives underpin your work as a team coach, why you do the work, and how those perspectives manifest themselves in the things you do as a team coach. Whatever questions help you gain clarity on those aspects of your practice are good questions.

In Chapters Five, Six, and Seven I covered some good ground in helping you formulate at least a first draft of your 3Ps for team coaching. You may remember my warning, not to treat the 3Ps as a one-off exercise, or some sort of test. We don't complete the 3Ps to define ourselves once and for all as a particular sort of team coach. So long as we remain committed to learning and to improving ourselves, so our 3Ps will continue to evolve and change. The structure reminds us to keep on exploring new approaches, and new ideas, to keep exploring who we are as human beings and how that manifests in the work that we do, to keep challenging ourselves as to why we do the work, to keep trying new things and reflecting on how we went. This is an ongoing reflective process.

I am using the word reflect a lot. I believe we must engage in an ongoing process of reflection to develop our practical judgment, and we must engage in reflection if we are to be clear, and continue being clear, as to the work we do and why we do it. To contemplate the 3Ps as a reflective process helps us segue into a conversation about supervision.

Supervision

I first came across the 3Ps model in a discussion around coaching supervision[1]. When I did my coach supervision training at Oxford Brookes University, I wasn't taught a list of competencies, I was introduced to the 3Ps model as a way of crystallising my work as a coach supervisor. This reflects how many coach supervisors there are out there, and how differently they all work. I have come across coach supervisors, including in the team coaching space, who evidently saw their role as being to educate me, or to provide me with tips and advice. My own approach to coaching supervision is to co-create a reflective space, in which supervisor and coachee can engage in dialogue in service of our learnings, and I will talk about supervision in this chapter through that lens.

The literature talks about three functions for supervision. Not every text uses exactly the same words. Here we'll refer to them as[2]:

Formative – facilitating personal and professional growth.
Normative – contributing to the quality of work and decision-making.
Restorative – providing emotional support.

In a study of 58 coaches undertaking group supervision, 100% said they came to supervision for the formative function, 84% said they came to supervision for the normative function, and 70% said they came for the restorative function[3]. From my own experience supervising team coaches, I would guess the balance to be more even across the board. I often work with team coaches, confused by all the different perspectives out there in the industry, wondering if they're doing a good job (normative), and my experience is similar to that of Alison Hodge and David Clutterbuck, who report that "every team coach we have encountered in our supervision practice has scars to show from early team coaching assignments, in which they were 'badly mauled,' which suggests a role for the restorative function."[4]

Based on a survey of 95 team coaches and team coach supervisors[5,6], Alison Hodge and David Clutterbuck conclude that the roles of a team coach supervisor include:

- Facilitating a substantial increase in skills, confidence, and ability to work with dynamic complexity.
- Expanding the coach's horizons, so that they address issues they didn't know they had.
- Helping the coach to reflect in such a way that they can gain deeper insights.

Alison Hodge talks also about[7]:

- Enabling the coach to gain clarity around their process and their task.
- Allowing the coach to bring more of themselves, their life experiences and wisdom into the space.

These roles align nicely with the potential value of the 3Ps, providing some early evidence that the 3Ps framework may prove useful in the team coaching supervision process.

Choosing a team coach supervisor

My prescription here is consistent with a leaning away from talking skills and competencies. The time you spend reflecting on your 3Ps will help you to gain fresh insights as to what new models and frameworks you may want to explore, to become more self-aware, and to decide what new methods you want to experiment with in practice. You will of course expect your team supervisor to be able to co-create the safe reflective space with you to explore some of these things, but what else emerges for you from this process in terms of the ideal team coach supervisor? If you have become fascinated by a certain way of working with team dynamics, then you may seek a supervisor who understands those models and has experience of putting them into practice. If you want to get better at contracting, which Hodge and Clutterbuck suggest is the cornerstone of the vast majority of team coaching supervision conversations, then you may seek out a supervisor who you feel will be able to help you especially in that space. Through this lens you may move supervisors from time to time, to access new perspectives in whatever area of practice you are most interested in, in-the-moment.

Hodge and Clutterbuck do however suggest some general attributes you may look for in a team coach supervisor, or that you may aspire toward as a potential coach supervisor. These include:

Experience

Your team coach supervisor may have great general supervision skills, but if their experience is limited in doing the work of a team coach, then you may not have access to a great example of practical judgment. Clutterbuck and Hodge surveyed 43 team coach supervisors[8]. Just under half had extensive experience themselves coaching teams. About a third had low to moderate experience. The less experienced team coach supervisor may be very good at creating the reflective space and may have a great breadth of knowledge in all the areas you are curious about, but they may have less practical judgment, less wisdom as to the challenges facing a team coach. This may or may not matter to you – only 27% of the team coaches surveyed by Clutterbuck and Hodge always separated out supervision for individual coaching from supervision for team coaching, suggesting a more general appetite for supervision.

An understanding of team dynamics

The importance of this aspect of team coaching will of course depend on your personal philosophy as to the relevance of team dynamics, though most team coaches do believe they need a good understanding of team process[9]. Hodge and Clutterbuck suggest that the potential for things to get out of control is far greater in team coaching because of the complexity of the relationships within a team. When I am in the room with one coachee, there is one relationship in the room. When I am working with a team of six people, there are 21 relationships in the room, including my relationships with team members. The work becomes exponentially more complex the more people there are in the room. I worked recently with a team of 13 people, which meant there were 91 relationships in the room. Regardless of my philosophical stance on working explicitly with team dynamics, it's hard to argue a case for not needing to have some informed perspective as to how those relationships may be functioning.

An understanding of systems

The Clutterbuck and Hodge survey suggests that many team coaches come to supervision looking for the opportunity to gain new ideas and awareness for working with the 'system'. The team coach supervisor must therefore have a good understanding of systems. Peter Hawkins also writes about the importance of being trained in 'systemic team coaching'[10]. I would say however, with reference to one of the debates in Chapter Three, that it isn't enough to talk about being systemic. There are lots of ways of being systemic.

Hodge and Clutterbuck say that supervisors must be able to take a systemic, as opposed to systematic, perspective of relationships and group dynamic. I don't personally like the distinction between systemic and systematic. Systemic thinking, Clutterbuck suggests, is about taking a holistic approach that views the team and its environment as interconnected and complex[11], whereas systematic thinking presumably describes a more methodical approach, more process-based, and linear. I don't much like the distinction, first because it is confusing. There are various systems that operate quite methodically, in a very linear fashion, a hot water system, for example. There are others that operate in a fashion that is quite obviously non-linear, weather systems, for example. And there are other systems whose functioning may appear linear or non-linear depending on your perspective on that system, or indeed that show signs of both. For me it is an oversimplistic, binary comparison. It implies there is the linear way of looking at things and there is a complex way of looking at things and the two are quite binary and distinct. Those who distinguish between systemic and systematic often seem to be drawing from some understanding of complexity. But there are various complexity theories, some of them quite linear, and hundreds of systems theories, and to categorise all these theories into two big buckets is too crude for my liking. The theories we pay attention to, that underpin our team coaching philosophy, drive the way we think and behave, and I believe we will make only limited progress in fully leveraging insights from the systems domain without a deeper exploration of those different ways of looking at the world. By now, of course, you will recognise this not as an objective critique of Clutterbuck's distinction, more as a manifestation of my own philosophy. Alison Hodge does elaborate upon her own philosophy in some detail. She discusses three related themes: systemic coaching as defined by Peter Hawkins, my own notion of meta-systems thinking, and Nora Bateson's writings on 'warm data'[12].

My point is – given that many of us see the need for team coaches to be 'systemic' – we need to further develop our understanding as to what that word can mean, in service of giving us access to new and useful ways of looking the world. And if that is your perspective too, then that may direct your choice of team coach supervisor.

These then are some thoughts on team coach supervision. I leave with you my own personal philosophy that supervision be regarded not only as a place to bring challenges and problems, but as a place to learn and grow more broadly. A place to develop that practical judgment, and to become more confident in going out to the world as a capable team coach.

Some of you may have read this chapter from a single relationship perspective. Individual team coach supervision is social, and it is useful, no doubt. People often choose to undertake individual supervision because it feels like the safest place to share thoughts, safer than any group[13]. In the old days, and still now in some domains, group supervision was seen principally as a more cost-effective, albeit less intense, opportunity to enjoy the benefits of supervision. Through this lens the supervisor is sometimes the 'master' and everyone else is there to benefit from that individual's wisdom. But the 3Ps framework reminds us how we can learn from *everyone* around us, be it our clients, our supervisors, our peers, or colleagues. Through this lens group supervision provides me with *multiple* perspectives, and accordingly more insights and inspiration in continuing to grow as a practitioner. Again, we don't need to choose which we prefer, individual or team supervision. We may engage in multiple forums, both formal and informal, in continuing to become the confident and capable wise team coach we aspire to be.

References

1. Jackson, P. & Bachkirova, T. (2019). The 3Ps of Supervision and Coaching: Philosophy, Purpose and Process. In: E. Turner & S. Palmer (Eds.), *The Heart of Coaching Supervision. Working with Reflection and Self-Care.* Routledge.
2. Notes from slides from *Professional Certificate in Coaching Supervision* program, Oxford Brookes University.
3. Lawrence, P. (2019). What Happens in Group Supervision? Exploring Current Practice in Australia. *International Journal of Evidence Based Coaching and Mentoring, 17(2)*, 138–157.
4. Hodge, A. & Clutterbuck, D. (2019). Supervising Team Coaches: Working with Complexity at a Distance. In: D. Clutterbuck, J. Gannon, S. Hayes, I. Iordanou, K. Lowe & D. Mackie (Eds.), *The Practitioner's Handbook of Team Coaching.* Routledge.
5. https://alisonhodge.com/wp-content/uploads/2020/03/team-coaching-supervision-survey-2017.pdf
6. Hodge, A. & Clutterbuck, D. (2019). Supervising Team Coaches: Working with Complexity at a Distance. In: D. Clutterbuck, J. Gannon, S. Hayes, I. Iordanou, K. Lowe & D. Mackie (Eds.), *The Practitioner's Handbook of Team Coaching.* Routledge.
7. Hodge, A. (2021). Supervising Team Coaches. In: T. Bachkirova, P. Jackson, D. Clutterbuck. *Coaching and Mentoring Supervision, 2nd edition.* McGraw Hill.
8. https://alisonhodge.com/wp-content/uploads/2020/03/team-coaching-supervision-survey-2017.pdf
9. Lawrence, P. & Whyte, A. (2014). What is Coaching Supervision and is it Important? *Coaching: An International Journal of Theory, Research and Practice, 7(1)*, 1–17.
10. Hawkins, P. (2011). *Leadership Team Coaching: Developing Collective Transformational Leadership.* Kogan Page.

11. Clutterbuck, D. (2007). *Coaching the Team at Work*. Nicholas Brealey.
12. Hodge, A. (2021). Supervising Team Coaches. In: T. Bachkirova, P. Jackson, D. Clutterbuck. *Coaching and Mentoring Supervision, 2nd edition*. McGraw Hill.
13. Lawrence, P. (2019). What Happens in Group Supervision? Exploring Current Practice in Australia. *International Journal of Evidence Based Coaching and Mentoring, 17(2)*, 138–157.

Conclusions

In the Introduction, I said this would be a different kind of book about team coaching. It was not my purpose to try and tell you how you should go about coaching teams, though no doubt aspects of my own 3Ps leaked out here and there, sometimes intentionally, other times by accident. But I hope you got the message, which was that in a complex, ever-changing and mysterious world, we cannot rely on others to provide us with simple rules to tell us how best to go about doing the work.

I hope you found some of the ideas presented here helpful. Others you may have found less inspiring, some you won't yet have found time to properly explore. I urge you to feel good about that. Being a team coach is not a traditional profession, a toolbox of practical skills we can go learn at college. Being a team coach is to develop a stronger sense of who we are as people, in relation to other people. To be able to simultaneously rise above ourselves whilst also participating in the day-to-day rough and tumble of working with groups of people.

This perspective reminds me of adult development theory, some of which ideas Suzi Skinner and I integrated into a model of wisdom[1]. It reminds me also of a conversation I had with Joel Monk from Coaches Rising[2]. In that podcast I shared with him some of the ideas from this book, above all the notion that we must craft our own developmental journeys and not overly invest in others' perspectives, including those framed as objective skills and competencies. As we talked, Joel wondered if there was a developmental lens to all this? Might it be that our dependent selves, those parts of us that look to others to tell us if we are doing the right thing, are most drawn to these standard frameworks, and most likely to align ourselves to someone else's particular model? Our more independent selves, those parts of ourselves able to refer to a solid sense of internal certainty, will more likely be drawn to constructing our own personal approaches, our own 3Ps. Our transcendent selves, akin to Robert Kegan's self-transforming selves[3], will be more comfortable holding that approach lightly, as an ongoing reference point, bound to evolve and change as it comes into contact with others' approaches. This part of me is not interested in defending my philosophies, purpose, and practice. Rather it is curious to understand your approach and open to integrating some of your 'stuff' in continuing to grow.

DOI: 10.4324/9781003546108-10

If this is a valid lens, then of course we cannot suddenly become the team coach we want to be. Our capacity to become great will be to an extent developmental. It will require us to engage in a never-ending journey of experimentation and reflection. As I said in the Introduction, I continue to find the job of team coaching very challenging, but also rewarding. I grow as a person through the work that I do, stepping outside my areas of certainty and comfort, to see what happens when working in a less familiar domain. The work is challenging, and it is rewarding.

I said I just about got out alive of my first team coaching assignment. In writing the book I went back to my notes for that assignment and, to my surprise, saw that not only did the overall assignment go for ten months, but it was adjudged a success by those with whom I worked. That's not how I remembered it. But as well as feeling like I fell flat on my face in the first session, I must have learned something too. Important to remember the good bits as well as the bad bits, another reminder perhaps, that we don't always need to take problems to supervision. We can take successes too and do our best to learn as much from those successes as we do hopefully from those experiences we think of as failures.

In this book I have explained how I was driven to overhaul my team coaching model a few years ago. I wonder why it took me so long? I think perhaps that my dependent self, wanting to feel safe and secure in the team coaching room, *was* looking for someone to tell me how to do it. It took me some time to realise that no one else's model was going to work best for me. I had some catching up to do, and so the exercise felt quite intense. My lesson from that has been to put aside anxiety and to stay curious. Alison Hodge and David Clutterbuck said that the people coming to team coaching supervision all had stories to tell about being 'badly mauled' in their early days of coaching teams[4]. I wonder if all those coaches were being entirely honest in attributing all the mauling to the early days. Does the mauling ever stop? Working as a group supervisor, I worked recently with a wonderful group of coaches over a four-year period who co-created a wonderful warm space in which to reflect together and share their experiences. They were all highly experienced coaches who still had bad days, especially when working with teams and groups. They didn't share those stories outside the group because they didn't trust everyone to hear those stories as examples of learning, rather than stories of being incompetent. The good news, I think, as we continue on our developmental journey, is that the mauling stops feeling like we are being mauled, and starts to feel more like a ball bouncing on the waves, being tossed and turned on stormy days, because that's what happens on stormy days, and we can all survive stormy days so long as we have someone to call upon to talk it all through, happy that the more stormy days we face, the better we get at doing the work.

I do urge you to find those people to continue your journey with. They may be fellow coaches, co-coaches, supervisors, whoever. But we learn best though our reflection with others, much more so than we do by attempting to learn on our own[5]. And seek to become wise. By that I mean make the time to reflect, get to know yourself better, find ways to rise above the work that you do, and take an elevated perspective. Be curious *and* be challenging. Ask questions and keep asking questions until you feel you have understood all there is to be understood. Or until the other person has enough and walks away. Resurrect the child within, always asking 'why?'

Whatever sense you made of the book, I hope you found it helpful, and I hope one day to hear about the journey you are on.

Paul Lawrence
paul@leadingsystemically.com

References

1. Lawrence, P. & Skinner, S. (2023). *The Wise Leader. A Practical Guide for Thinking Differently About Leadership.* Routledge.
2. www.coachesrising.com/podcast/the-field-of-team-coaching-with-paul-lawrence/
3. Kegan, R. (1998). *In Over Our Heads. The Mental Demands of Modern Life.* Harvard University Press.
4. Hodge, A. & Clutterbuck, D. (2019). Supervising Team Coaches: Working with Complexity at a Distance. In: D. Clutterbuck, J. Gannon, S. Hayes, I. Iordanou, K. Lowe & D. Mackie (Eds.), *The Practitioner's Handbook of Team Coaching.* Routledge.
5. Lawrence, P. & Skinner, S. (2023). *The Wise Leader. A Practical Guide for Thinking Differently About Leadership.* Routledge.

Appendix

1. I work with teams to enable them to realise their own wisdom and experience in order to operate as more than the sum of their parts.
2. I know what bad looks like, and even in a position of influence felt powerless. I had to go. I want nobody to have to go through that. That drives me. Equity, fairness, being a good human.
3. My why is a deep desire to share my abilities on behalf of a community (in this case a team), so we can collectively witness the true nature of 'learning', 'creating', and 'making a difference' together.
4. To accelerate team cohesion and team development.
5. Because fundamentally I believe we can achieve more together than we do alone. Given the nature of challenges we face as a species, as organisations, and as teams, working together effectively is a necessity.
6. I coach teams because I recognize the profound potential that lies within collective human endeavour. My deeper purpose stems from a belief in the inherent goodness of people and the transformative power of collaboration. At my core, I am driven by the vision of mending a fragmented society and fostering an environment where 'togethering' (coming together to work side by side) becomes the norm rather than the exception. My ultimate goal is to overcome the pervasive 'story of separation' that plagues modern society. By guiding teams to operate cohesively and harmoniously, I aim to demonstrate that true progress, real, meaningful progress, emerges from cooperation and mutual support. I am not just building better teams; I am nurturing a cultural shift towards interconnectedness, empathy, and shared purpose. In a broader sense, I want to positively affect i) human connection and understanding. By fostering collaboration, I help people understand and appreciate each other's perspectives, reducing division and fostering a sense of unity. ii) Personal and collective growth. I aim to unlock the potential within each individual and the collective team, promoting continuous learning, self-improvement, and collective achievement. iii) Societal healing. Hopefully, my work is a step towards healing societal wounds, bridging gaps between diverse groups, and creating a more inclusive and equitable world. iv) Sustainable progress.

I envision a future where progress is not driven by competition and individualism but by sustainable, cooperative efforts that benefit all members of society.

7. I am really only working with one team where I would say it is team coaching. I support them with their annual planning meeting each November which is a two to three-day workshop and mid-year we normally do a one or two day workshop which is part business review and part leadership development. My role is to i) facilitate the business agenda and to offer my observations as to dynamics I notice in relation to creative and reactive behaviours that might emerge during the working through of the business dynamics, and ii) we normally do some leadership development. Initially we did a two-day workshop debriefing our 360 reports. Then a six-hour peer coaching course, followed by two × three hours coaching modules. Then over the years we do two to three online modules including emotional intelligence, the power of vulnerability, growth mindset, peer coaching with each other, conflict management, crucial conversations, collaboration, etc. Managing stages of team dynamics. Then there have been a number of online three-four hour modules where we explore a topic, discuss where we see it at play, I offer a couple of models or concepts, then we the move into groups of three to peer-coach using the iGROW model. In this context I define the 'i'.

8. I do team coaching because supporting the development of high-performing teams is very important for organisations and its staff members. Individual coaching is good for developing certain leadership and other skills, but the dynamic of teams requires a different kind of capability. Team coaching enables members to examine their effectiveness in achieving true synergistic outcomes – and trialling different approaches to achieve better outcomes along the way. Hopefully, the learning can be translated back into truly effective team outcomes across the organisation.

9. I want to be of service to the group and sometimes being in the coach role allows for the team to see themselves with a different perspective.

10. I'll start with a quote from Foucault: "People know what they do; frequently they know why they do what they do; but what they don't know is what what they do does." I wanted to start with this quote as your question got me thinking about the function of team coaching. Here, I have two main questions: what are the effects of team coaching and how can we trace them? What is its utility? For whom? I won't answer these questions. I've been noticing the complexity turn in a lot of theorising. Delueze and Guttari wrote a book a while ago called 'A thousand plateaus'. Here, they introduce a couple of key ideas that I think have some utility as metaphors for complexity. One is the rhizome. A rhizome is a botanical term. Rhizomes pop out of the ground over an expanding area making it seem like separate plants are growing. But these individual plants are just part of one big plant. In Deleuze and Guattari's work, rhizome is the philosophical counterpart of the botanical term. They suggest

that political, economic, social, and organisational forms and structures are rhizomatically interconnected and conjoined though such connections are not always visible (they rarely are). They describe key characteristics of rhizomes (or horizontal network connections). The first is connectivity and heterogeneity. Every part of the system is connected to another part in any possible way. The second is multiplicity. In a rhizome, all the parts are connected to one another and these to others. It is distributed, without a centre. It has no beginning or end. I think that teams are always already rhizomes; characterized by multiplicity, connectivity, and heterogeneity. I've heard coaching and therapy being described as a holding environment. This is usually described in fairly humanistic terms (safe space, etc.). However, I think the term can be repurposed for team coaching if we see teams as rhizomes (always connected to every other part) and team coaching as a holding environment where teams are afforded the opportunity to engage in connectivity and heterogeneity. The metaphor of a rhizome is useful for coaches. If teams are a part of 'one plant' all teams will ultimately show similar characteristics. All of this is an attempt to answer your question. My purpose for team coaching is that I think it may be a useful practice in helping teams develop. Not in the humanistic sense of the term, but the rhizomatic. To make visible and build other connections, to look at heterogeneity and where necessary, to produce rupture connections to develop new connections.

11. I choose to work as a team coach because it amplifies the impact I can have within an organisation, and frankly it's both challenging and fun. Working with leaders to effectively leverage their teams is extremely fulfilling. Many leaders struggle to do this on their own, so having a coach to help lighten the load is usually greatly appreciated. And who doesn't want to be appreciated? If I focus on my purpose, it is simple – to enable leaders and their teams to achieve their potential. To facilitate their self-awareness, and other leadership skills, and help them hold themselves accountable.

12. I coach teams to help them be the best they can be and achieve their mission, purpose, and objectives and I enjoy the dynamics and energy from team coaching.

13. To enable teams to work better together to achieve their collective purpose.

14. The reason I do team coaching is to provide an environment where the team members can resolve an issue/build a process/develop their skills/reflect on their behaviours so that they come to an understanding of what may be holding them (as a team or as an individual) back in a team and provide an opportunity for team members to use their strengths. The reason I do team coaching is to discover understand/provide understanding/challenge understanding on how they see their team linking to the organisation. How do they make sense of the organisational/environmental system? I do not like to do any coaching if it feels 'outside' the organisation. It needs to be linked to the organisation's strategy and values.

15. To enable the team collectively and the individuals therein to connect with trust and care, to build relationships that are secure and psychologically safe and authentic and, as such, to work better, more productively, more seamlessly, together. To help teams understand their team and individual strengths such that they support each other differently and without fear of not being able to do everything which is neither sustainable nor real.

16. To create space to surface behaviours and other dynamics so that the team can see them and decide what, if anything, to do about them.

17. To facilitate the growth of the team towards a better understanding of working better together. By expanding the team's mindsight, the team moves beyond the toxic patterns of entrenched behaviours.

18. The biggest distinction is between group coaching and team coaching – and most of the time the client doesn't understand the difference. I'd say most of the time when I've been asked to conduct team coaching, it was actually group coaching. So much of this discussion begins with defining a team. Are they really a team? In true teams, there is a requirement for interdependence in order to reach a shared goal. Each person has a unique role or skill to contribute, creating a systemic outcome that none could have achieved individually. Often I'm asked to coach 'sales teams' and must begin with the idea of 'you are not a team, you're a group'.

19. To amplify the impact I can have through coaching. I have experienced seeing significant change and positive development in my one-on-one counterparts. Through team coaching this impact is amplified and goes to creating a culture within a team that can also foster the development of the individual. I also believe that through developing teams you can have a positive impact on an organisation and through the team make change and create better cultures. With the current state of workplace disengagement, lack of belonging, and worker burnout I believe developing teams to be better and do better through coaching, it is the good teams that can create cultures where employees are engaged, they belong, and avoid burning out, whilst still delivering good outcomes for the organisations they serve.

20. I do team coaching in the hope I can make some small positive impact in the terrible results we see annually in the Gallup 'State of Work' report. Life at work should not be having such a negative impact on people's well-being.

21. To help the teams I work with actually become teams and therefore improve the way they deliver their work. Most teams I am asked to help are not actually teams at all, and they only need to have the capability when they need it for larger challenges.

22. My purpose is primarily vertical developmental growth of the individuals through the constructionism of the social group context. Vygotsky's social and proximal learning is a good frame. Community building as opposed to team building through thinking together as opposed to activities together. Group events off-site attempt to be a proxy for reality and for me the preferred proxy is novel dialogue as opposed to novel activities.

23. Simply put, to effectively help the team develop more characteristics of a high-performing team.
24. My purpose is to help teams focus on what matters and to create change from within, with an underlying belief that when teams slow down and consider what matters, quality relationships and meaningful impact rises up.
25. My reason for coaching (organisations/teams/individuals) is to have a positive global impact on patients' health (live better, longer/more people) and, at the same time help my clients and me become better versions of ourselves. Personally, it's about my spiritual growth.
26. An element of team coaching that is unique is the opportunity to work with the psychodynamics and paradoxes of team and group life. If a team is prepared to go that way, it can open up all sorts of possibilities for change and development.
27. I came to team coaching as an extension of my c-suite individual coaching when I realised the only place I could see my client 'perform' was to be with them in their team meetings. Then I realised I could help them be more effective if I could help the team be more effective. My purpose has always been the same. How do I help leaders maximise their effectiveness? The same applies for leadership teams. The cascading effect down the organisation can be very powerful.
28. My purpose is strongly aligned to collective team commitment to being values driven in creating value for and with all stakeholders present and future.
29. The primary purpose is to facilitate and enhance the performance and cohesion of the team by understanding and addressing the interconnected elements and dynamics that influence the team's performance and overall environment. I tend to look at team dynamics, organisational and wider context, individual contributions, team processes, and external influences. So that's the formal answer. Truth is though, I'm deeply interested in how we evolve (or not) as systems and what are the environmental factors that we can co-create that lead to increased performance, trust and psychological safety, thereby leading to healing for all involved.
30. Intuitively it seems like the next step forward from individual leadership coaching, it provides some variety and new challenges. My purpose is to add value in alignment with the intentions and best interests of the team whom I am coaching. Purpose feels a little self-indulgent, abstract, and pointless at this point. We are all f****d. Do no harm, be honest, and add value to help unlock communication, dialogue, performance, value, kindness, relationships, etc.
31. My purpose for team coaching is to contribute to a future where everyone has the opportunity to be part of a team that learns, grows, and laughs together whilst doing some great work. Bonus points if each team member also feels a genuine sense of belonging in the team and connection to the team purpose. Bonus points if the team is aligned to the organisation's interests and needs.

Super bonus points (my own private mission) – team coaching cultivates love where fear once lived.

32. I do team coaching when a client can see the team can benefit from exploring issues as a team rather than as individuals and when individuals in a team are confident they can identify what they want from the coaching.

33. My purpose is to facilitate more productive interactions among the team members such that i) the experience of participation in the team is more positive, and ii) because the interactions are better (both safer and more direct), the resulting productivity and efficacy of the team is improved.

34. To help a team take perspective, be challenged and supported and to shift difficult and often stuck patterns of team behaviour affecting their performance.

35. The empowerment of others through self-realisation and active, interconnected co-creation that develops them as self-determined learners.

36. I do team coaching because of my belief in the wisdom that teams hold, and often, that is underrated. My purpose is to unleash the team's wisdom so that it realises its potential by taking progressive action.

37. I do team coaching as it offers me a level of challenge beyond individual work. I am drawn to complex work, and the challenge in working with human systems. I also believe deeply in team coaching, and my training supports the power of working systemically and not just individually. I also do team coaching as it helps me/our business differentiate and grow in a competitive landscape. Clients 'know' to come here for quality team coaching, so for sure part of the motivation to do team coaching is that it supports building a thriving business.

38. To enhance a functioning (hopefully well-functioning but depends where they start from) team to enable better quality of life and effective working and relationships for coachees and enhance effectiveness of experience and outcomes for patients and colleagues.

39. My fundamental purpose in team coaching is to ensure that teams are supported and challenged to share leadership with one another, where every voice is heard, perspectives are voiced respectfully and collectively, they are given the opportunity to grow through each other, in service of amplifying their positive impact. Through confidential team dialogue and collective reflective practices, each team is enabled to create a safe space to explore their collective growth opportunities and the areas where their positive impact matters the most. My purpose is grounded in the belief that aligned teams who share a common purpose, can change the world for the better. This positive impact orientation underpins my approach and philosophy of working with teams wherever they are on the planet.

40. To strengthen the relationships between the team members. Give them the opportunity to be working on team challenges and successes together. Support each other, coach each other, increase insights, help get a better (broader and deeper) view of the system they are working in away from the pressure of

BAU from the outside looking in. Creating the pause to observe and reflect on a regular basis.

41. I typically do team coaching with teams that are not functioning particularly well and it is having a negative impact on the business. All my interventions are centred around helping the business to be as high-performing as possible. As part of this work, it can become evident that the business's or function's performance challenges are due to the dysfunctional team. The focus is to help them recognise the unhelpful patterns, commit to changing them, and to find common ground that they can all rally behind. The purpose is to re-set the team's ground rules and introduce techniques that will allow them to have the discussions and make the right decisions while changing the team's culture to a more useful one.

42. To facilitate executive teams so that they decide and then execute on:

   - Why do they exist – why do they come together?
   - What work they are meant to do together that they cannot do as individuals.
   - What each individual's accountability is to every member of the team and the team itself, and how to activate and review the effectiveness of their accountabilities.
   - What processes they use and how these can be improved.
   - How to increase the trust between each pair of members of the team.
   - How to integrate strategy with execution, with team and organisational culture, and each person's development within the team context.

43. Overall my purpose is to support clients to take personal responsibility for where they may find themselves and to establish the best course of action to forward that which best serves whatever is most effective for them, their life, and the system they belong to. My fascination is in how patterns or themes that may have been formed from our lives to date can keep showing up, and unless we recognise our co-creation in those patterns, there is little anyone else can do to shift them. All relationships create dynamics and patterns – they have a life of their own, and the system or relational dynamic can constrain the individuals within. I love to help people locate themselves within the system or relational dynamic that they are caught in and help them to determine what is constrained within them and increase awareness and choice over how they want to show up as best as they can. My work is underpinned by Kantor's model, and systemic thinking, and in essence helps teams to 'see the system' they have created, be empowered to determine what they want or need from themselves or altogether as they face into different contexts, for most effective performance and outcomes and in a timely manner.

44. Collaborative inquiry, all voices and perspectives heard when approaching complex workplace challenges and goals. Elevate the individual and collective capacity of a team in a way that is creative, collaborative, and developmental.

45. Team coaching is about helping teams achieve some form of change. So, my purpose in team coaching is to help teams effect their desired change, whatever that may look like.

46. I believe we are created for relationships. Teams are one of the many ways people experience relationships in a work context. I team coach to improve and accelerate cohesive relationships in teams. When teams have strong relationships they work better together, improve their outcomes, and achieve more. This is good for the organisation and it's good for the employees. It is rewarding for me to see this shift and to know I've made a difference.

47. With the clients that I serve, many of their efforts and initiatives require shifts and changes to the systems, the culture, even the processes of the organization. This, by its very nature, is larger than the capability of any one individual to do on their own. Team coaching places the emphasis squarely on the dynamics of a team-based, collective endeavour, relative to varying levels of systemic order, to succeed at implementing a new idea, a new change, a new initiative, a different way of collective (and individual) being.

48. There are a few reasons why I work with teams. First, to facilitate a change process that can enable a team to move towards a state of working and performing towards 'better'. Second, to develop the team's capacity to build their teaming and team coaching skills so they can develop a way to observe and regulate their performance towards better within their team and within the organisation. Three, because I enjoy working with teams – it's fun, interesting, and enjoyable. Each team interaction builds my own understanding and appreciation of human connections.

Index

Printed in the United States
by Baker & Taylor Publisher Services